Bulletproof Principles
For
Personal Success

Charleene!

Enjoy the Book!

9/25/03

Bulletproof Principles
For
Personal Success

Michael Schlappi

Library of Congress Cataloging-in Publication Data:
Schlappi, Michael P.
Bulletproof Principles for Striking Gold

ISBN 1-928845-17-7
First paperback edition revised and expanded 2001

Second paperback edition revised 2003
with new title:
Bulletproof Principles for Personal Success

Cover design by Richard Ferguson
Text design by Sheryl Mehary

10 9 8 7 6 5 4 3

Please inquire about our quantity discount schedule

Dedication

To those who dedicate their lives to help others. For me, this means my wife Tami, our incredible kids, and of course my parents and siblings. And to my close friends who have become part of my extended family through the experiences we have shared.

Love, Mike

Acknowledgments

My deepest gratitude to all of you
who have touched my life
and enriched my days
I could not have done it without you.

Michael Schlappi

Contents

Introduction

Every man or woman who has been
- challenged to overcome a personal defeat;
- overwhelmed by a crushing loss;
- brought to that low point when everything seems dull, grey and flat;
- worried about the future and needs inspiration to raise self-confidence and to revive courage,

will find answers in the remarkable story of Paralympic gold medalist Michael Schlappi. Out of disaster, he found the strength, courage and determination to triumph over life's uncertainties and to build a successful future of outstanding achievements.

A terrifying injury and a shock too deep for tears shattered young Mike's promising future when he was just fourteen, leaving him bereft of his dearest expectation of a career in sports as a top American athlete. The bullet that immobilized him one fall day in 1977, almost took his life and certainly wrote the tragic aftermath for his best friend who accidentally pulled the trigger of his father's pistol.

Mike's story is not just one of his recovery from a horrible wound that confined him to a wheelchair for the rest of his life. It goes much deeper than that, for it captures a rare, but universal and inextinguishable valor that resides in each of us. It comes to the surface when an individual has the courage and tenacity to reach far down into the soul and discover the wellspring of our humanness — which comes from God.

It was this understanding of the latent power within each of us and the willingness to engage it in his own behalf that convinced Michael he did not have to give in to his injury, limit his grasp on the world or turn his mind and imagination away from what he wanted most to be.

In the twenty-five years since Mike was paralyzed, his life has become, as former President Bill Clinton remarked, "A great accomplishment achieved in an all-American way. He is an inspiration to people everywhere who want to succeed."

Mike's success has been notable. He is a two-time Paralympic Gold Medal winner and the only wheelchair basketball player to compete and earn medals in four consecutive Paralympic Games, in Seoul, Barcelona, Atlanta and Sydney. Mike is honored by his home state of Utah as one of its Top 50 Athletes of the Twentieth Century, and he served on the Board of Trustees for the 2002 Olympic Games in Salt Lake City.

But success means more to Mike than to be honored at the White House, or admired by audiences around the world he addresses on the *Unconquerable Power of the Human Spirit to Rise above Adversity.*

This is the strong message that emerges from his personal story and it is the one, Mike believes, that is crucial for Americans to embrace during a troubling time of international upheaval and threat.

Readers discover in *Bulletproof Principles for Personal Success* a gripping narrative of a young man's loss, the strengthened re-emergence of his will to fight back and to refocus his purpose in a passion to live, to grow, and change. He realized that this was the challenge he must accept almost immediately after he recovered from the surgery to repair his body from the bullet's damage. In order to live, to grow, and change, Mike had to find a "mental Windex" to regain his clarity of vision.

Discovering this clarity deep inside himself and stubbornly building upon it, the Six Bulletproof Principles for Success he developed, led Mike over many obstacles to achievements which he describes in his book. The result has been a record of success accurately expressed by Mike's friend, United States Senator Orrin Hatch, who said, "Mike Schlappi's life teaches anyone who has ever thought that the mountain was too high, or the valley was too wide, that the will of the human heart can conquer all obstacles."

Chapter 1

The Shot that Changed My World

I remember, as if it were yesterday how excited I was about picking up my friend and heading out with him to the football field at Lakeridge Junior High where we both went to school. We lived on the same street in Orem, Utah, about four houses apart.

I was really looking forward to the game that afternoon and when I left my house, the screen door flew open behind me and slapped against the side of the house. Instantly, I leaped down the three front steps and quickly cut right as if I was dodging a tackle in the approaching championship game. My football cleats dug into the freshly-cut lawn as I raced through two neighbors' yards, then across the road to my friend's house.

Today was a great day, one I had looked forward to for months. Our team had survived the Little League All-Star football playoffs and for the championship we were to play our cross-county rivals from Provo. Three weeks shy of my fifteenth birthday, I had been blessed with unusual coordination. Because I was the quarterback of the team, and was responsible for leading the team to victory, I was pretty serious about my role. It wasn't something I gloated about, but inwardly I felt fortunate — an athlete with promise and potential.

When I arrived at Torrey's house, I rapped solidly on the door. I was feeling ten feet tall, and my adrenaline was pumping so fast I could hardly wait to get to the ball field. I had never been accused of having patience, especially when I had to wait for a big game to begin.

"Come in; the door's open!" Torrey called from the back bedroom. I entered the house and headed in the direction of his voice. He was still getting dressed, so I just sauntered around. The grass clippings on my cleats had left a path from the front door to his parents' bedroom, and continued to leave traces wherever I walked. But I was a fourteen-year-old boy, and as such was oblivious to the mess I was making.

Sitting finally on the edge of the bed, I looked curiously around and noticed his father's .38 caliber revolver on the night-stand. This was not out of the ordinary, however, because Torrey's dad, Lou Fetheroff, was a police officer and this was his off-duty pistol.

Boys are fascinated with guns and I had grown up in a household that made game hunting a high priority during deer and pheasant season. I leaned over and picked up the pistol. It was in a brown leather case, and the flap was snapped closed. My only thought was how heavy it was.

By this time, my friend was nearly ready to go. He came into the bedroom where I was holding his father's revolver, and smiled. "Hi, Mike! Ready to kick some Provo butt?!"

As my friend spoke, he reached over and took the gun from my hands. He then unsnapped the leather cover, while I plopped down on the bed in anticipation of getting a closer look at such a magnificent weapon. Without speaking, he flipped open the cylinder. I watched, transfixed, as the stainless steel bullets fell harmlessly to the bed. One, two, three, four … five. I counted the bullets as they lazily bounced onto the white bedspread. They looked cool, all silver and sleek. I remember thinking, how many bullets does the gun hold?

Then, Torrey pushed the cylinder closed with his hand, and held the gun up. Knowing the gun was now empty, he was simply playing around with it. Innocently, he pointed the gun at my chest and pulled the trigger. That instant — that agonizing, life-altering split second — became the most serious and mentally replayed moment in each of our lives. Its repercussion was immediate, although it would be months and even years before either of us would feel its full impact. Fortunately for me, the consequences would be positive, for they would set me on a course of destiny that contained blessings and promises unfathomed.

The .38 caliber bullet that struck me tore a massive hole through my shirt, ripped into my chest and propelled me violently against the headboard of the bed. My body convulsed and shook with the shock while my mind struggled to comprehend. Unbeknownst to me, the bullet brushed past my heart, then slammed into my back-bone, causing me to instantly lose all comprehension of feeling.

"Quit kidding around!" Torrey screamed, while at the same time throwing the gun toward the corner of the room.

"Quit it! You're faking it! Get up … you're faking it!"

What's happening? I asked myself. *Why is he screaming? Why can't I breathe?*

As these questions seemed to rise in slow motion in my confused mind, I grabbed my shirt and pulled it up for Torrey to see. The wound was staggering and the blood was spreading across my chest. Taking in the damage, Torrey ran from the room in shocked terror. I could hear him in the living room crying and mumbling and throwing things around in frantic disbelief. I tried to call out to him to phone my mom, but it was hard for me to breath. I reached for the phone on the bedside table to call her, but … my legs wouldn't respond, and even more confusion ensued. Although I didn't realize it at that moment, the bullet had pierced my right lung, and breathing was becoming almost impossible.

My lung was collapsing and strangely, I could feel it filling with blood. My whole body seemed heavy, glued to the bed, waiting for my next command, yet conscious that it could not respond. I was becoming increasingly dizzy and lightheaded … and while I could hear my friend yelling and throwing dishes in the kitchen, and pounding on the organ keys in disbelief, my only thought was that if I was to survive he had to call my mom in the next few minutes.

Reaching down with my right hand, I grasped my thigh. But there was no feeling. I tilted my head to my right, and looked down along my body to confirm my greatest fears. Although I could sense a tingling sensation inside my leg, there was no feeling at all from the contact my hand had made on my clothes and skin.

Time was almost suspended, and while it seemed like an eternity, sixty to ninety seconds later my friend reentered the room and hunched down next to me. There was panic in his eyes as he grabbed my shoulders and shook me as if I was playing a horrible joke on him. When it finally dawned on him that I was terribly wounded he picked up the phone and dialed my number at home.

While his words floated through my puzzled mind, my initial response was, *Why me? I'm an athlete ... I need my legs!* I just didn't get it.

Moments passed, and soon I blacked out. Somewhere in the midst of this nightmare of increasing pain, I promised God that if He would let me live, I would be a better person; and I would share my experiences with the world. How much of this I promised at that moment, I really don't know. What I do know is that my mind became increasingly fuzzy, and then the lights went out.

My next recollection was being wheeled on a stretcher into the emergency room of the local hospital. The doctors were hovering over me, examining my chest; and were telling my mother it was probable that I would not survive the next few hours. It was that point-blank. At that instant I knew that I was on the brink of losing my life. Barring a miracle if I managed to be saved, I would be spending the rest of my life in a wheelchair. Gone were the sports activities which were the passion of my life.

I remember thinking, as I saw my mother's worried face before the door to the emergency room shut her out, how much I loved her and how her comforting presence helped me hang on. Her being there made me think that everything was going to turn out alright. She more than proved her love for me in the months of uncertainty that followed.

Later I read her version of what happened to me on that Friday early in November of 1977 from the diary she wrote. I was fascinated because she described the events more reliably than I remembered them. I've chosen excerpts from what she put down because I think they make the story I'm telling more vivid and accurate:

On Friday, November 11, Michael was out of school because of a Parent-Teachers Union Conference. Earlier in the morning he had been on hand as student body president at Lakeridge Junior High School. He was host to the parents. He came home and fixed his and his sister Julie's bike tires. About 2:30 P.M., he skipped over to his friend Torrey Fetheroff's house. Mike had been chosen as an All-Star Football player and he had gone over to get Torrey for an important game.

About 3:00 P.M., I was getting ready for a church dinner that night when the phone rang. I heard Torrey's voice yelling on the other end of the line, "Mrs. Schlappi, come quick, Mike's been hurt!"

I said, "What's wrong?" Torrey replied, "Just hurry!" I then knew that it was urgent and I ran out of the door shouting to my sister, Janet, who was visiting: "Mike's been hurt. I've got to run!"

I jumped in the Suburban and drove over to Torrey's house, which was only about three houses north of ours. Torrey met me at the door telling me Mike was in the back bedroom. I ran to him and there he was laying on the bed. He had his shirt pulled up exposing his chest. He said, "Mother, I've been shot! I can't breathe, and I can't move my legs."

My heart was in my mouth and I got a terrible sick feeling. I told Mike to lay quietly, I would call the ambulance. Mike seemed alert and calm, in good control and that helped me think more clearly. Torrey was running through the house screaming and going out of his head. He was in shock. I could hear Mike calling to him. "It's okay Torrey!"

I called the ambulance but I couldn't get Torrey settled enough to give me the exact house address. Finally, I got what I needed from him and ran back into Michael. By then Janet had followed me on foot to see what was happening and we both stood by Michael to comfort him while we were waiting for the ambulance. I remember the scared feelings I had racing through my mind. I kept trying to figure out where the heart is located.

Janet and I didn't want to move him because he had no feelings in his legs. In the background, I could hear Torrey still screaming and tearing around the house.

I was astonished at how fast the ambulance and paramedics arrived. One of the first policemen to come through the door was Torrey's father who was on duty at the time. The first thing the paramedics did was to straighten Michael out on the bed and check his vital signs. They knew right away he had a collapsed lung. He was in a lot of pain by then, but was still cooperative. Quickly the medics got some oxygen into Mike and called for the stretcher. I learned from their examination that the bullet was still in Mike's back.

Just then Michael's father, Larry, arrived and helped to put Mike on the stretcher.

I realized I was now in shock. They put Mike in the ambulance and asked us to ride in the police car. Bishop Richard Jones of our church rode with us. My daughter, Jennifer, who was only four, tried to grab me as we got in and finally a neighbor took her. I noticed a man there with a camera, a newsman I guess, and also the street, of course, was filled with curious and concerned neighbors.

The ride seemed forever in the police car, even though we moved quickly through traffic. When we arrived at the hospital, Mike was already in the emergency room. They were treating his lung, ordering x-rays, watching his blood pressure and pulse. In all the anxiety, the admission clerks kept asking us questions. Larry and I couldn't even think.

Finally, the neurosurgeon, Dr. Kirkpatrick, arrived. He examined Michael, studied the x-rays and then started testing him for feeling. There was still no feeling in him from his waist down. It was about this time that Mike began having terrific stomach cramps. My mother, Mary Palmer, arrived at the hospital at this time. I also remember Rex Skinner being there. He introduced himself as the detective assigned to the case. The general surgeon also was there and he made an incision in Mike's right side about four inches down from the armpit and inserted a tube to drain the blood from the lung and chest cavity.

The neurosurgeon finally called Larry and me into a side room and reviewed the x-rays with us. He showed us that it appeared the bullet had damaged the spinal column and was now just lodged in some fatty tissue. Dr. Kirkpatrick was so blunt and cold with his facts, I just knew he couldn't be right, even though he explained in detail what the x-rays were showing. The general surgeon who was friendlier, told us Mike's vital signs were fair but they couldn't explain how the bullet ever missed Mike's heart, having taken the path that it did.

We were told by the doctors that if Mike could hang on in intensive care for the next 24 to 36 hours he would have a good chance of making it.

I never knew I could ever love a child so much as I did at that moment. I wanted to do anything I could to help him. The next time we talked to the neurosurgeon he told us he had spoken to Mike and told him he might never walk again. When I heard this I thought how cruel to tell a young boy who was desperately fighting for his life that he may be a cripple if he did survive.

The doctor also told us that there was one chance in a million that Mike could recover use of his legs if feeling returned to them within three or four days. He explained that when a bullet is involved, the intensity of the shock wave to the body could paralyze.

After that consultation we knew that it would take a miracle for Mike to walk again. We tried so hard to understand. Why? Why Mike? Why did this happen to us, to Mike? Finally, we were able to ask Mike what really happened? The story Torrey had related was different from the real truth. The version we heard on the radio when we were riding in the police car was that Mike's wound was self-inflicted. Of course, his dad and I both knew Mike had been taught well about gun safety. But after hearing Mike's own story when he was strong enough to tell us, we knew Torrey had lied. We were certain it was not to shift blame from himself to Mike. It was the desperate act of a boy afraid to admit to his policeman father that he'd been careless with his father's off-duty gun. Torrey had told his dad that Mike shot himself when he tried to put the gun in the nightstand. We knew that was false because

Mike was lying at the top of the bed unable to move his legs and the pistol and bullets were resting on the bottom of the bed five feet from Mike.

We told Detective Rex Skinner the real story and Torrey finally admitted the truth. He badly needed to get the heavy burden of his lie off his chest.

What made both of us feel good was the knowledge that Mike harbored no feelings of hatred for his good friend. His father and I never really felt any anger for the boy, knowing that a human error had been committed and so often the innocent are the ones to suffer.

Saturday, the day Mike was supposed to play in the football game with Torrey he was still stabilizing after a long night of careful monitoring. The physicians had placed a tube in his right lung to drain the blood and watch for internal bleeding. His stomach was beginning to ache with awful pain. The doctor explained that his nervous system had been so shocked that it was now super sensitive. Mike was given a Demerol shot every four hours. It gave him relief for an hour or two and then wore off. It was so bad that he screamed if his stomach was touched by a bed sheet. I know he appreciated how terrific the intensive care nurses were at Utah Valley Hospital. They were so understanding and went out of their way to make Mike more comfortable and happy.

By Saturday night, Mike was alert enough to watch Brigham Young University play Arizona State on TV in a contest to decide the WAC Conference football title. Mike was moved across the hall so he could watch the game. We sat with him until we knew he was tiring.

———◆———

My mother's diary not only clarified the sequence of events following the shooting, but helped me recall my feelings about how I would handle my altered life. Dozens of questions about my future popped into my head as I slowly healed.

Thoughts like these came to my mind: Will my friends accept me? Will girls like me? Will I ever get a normal job? Will they send me to some special home where people take care of me for the rest of my life? Even more basic to me was, Does God still love me?

These thoughts sound crazy when I think about them now, but they actually ran through my head following my accident because I had never known anyone personally who was in a wheelchair, other than people I would see getting pushed around the mall in wheelchairs — usually older people, not 14-year-olds.

I was in a lot of physical pain because my back hurt where the bullet struck my spine. I also had — and still have — a lot of phantom pains (they seem real to me) where the nerves in my belly and legs feel like they are on fire. Even more, I was in mental pain with so many worries and uncertainties. So, "Attitude Therapy," the title I came up with to describe the positive outlook I developed, helped me to stay upbeat and focus on the good things I had left. I often say that I used to be able to do 10,000 things and now I can only do 9,900. As a joke, I will say that the only things I can't do are things like dishes, laundry, and toilets. I think the world — even the medical professionals — are beginning to realize what I discovered, and that is that your body will heal quicker if your spirit and attitude are in good shape.

From my mother's diary I learned another fact about those who are seriously injured. The pain and misery are so great that the healing process completely absorbs you. You forget most of the details. After I was discharged from the hospital I learned a lot about the ordeal I went through from what my mother recorded on a daily basis. I also learned how important it is to have family and friends gather around you to show their love and support. My mom put this in perspective when she wrote the following:

———

"I can't begin to acknowledge the gratitude I felt for all the people who made Mike's recovery a priority in their lives, and I thought to myself again and again how insignificant everything I was doing prior to Mike's accident. After all, people are the most important thing here on this earth. Our testimonies, how we feel, how we help other people must be the main plan of our Heavenly Father.

Sunday and Monday Mike was able to eat a little bit. He was given liquids the first two days. A pain in his back caused great concern. The doctors explained that it came from the injury caused by the bullet damaging nerves. He cautioned us that the pain could last two weeks, two months, or forever. Also, Dr. Gaufin, the neurosurgeon now treating Mike, answered our questions and explained the medical aspects of what had happened to him. He told us that if Mike progresses as well as he was doing now, he could be moved from Intensive Care on Tuesday, and on Friday, he should be transferred to Holy Cross Hospital in Salt Lake City. There rehabilitation would begin. Dr. Gaufin also informed us that every hour that passes without sensation returning to his legs, reduces the chance of Mike regaining the use of them.

Tuesday Mike was moved to a regular room. He was so glad to have a phone and enjoyed talking to his friends. He was delighted when one of his favorite teachers and fifteen of his classmates came to his room. They hung a poster on one wall with everyone's signature written on it. It was about eight or nine feet in size. Mail was pouring in for Mike. The student council brought him a plant in a basketball planter. That night kids from his school just flocked into his room. So many, in fact, that the nurse reported they were jamming the elevators and crowding the halls. It was a great treat for Mike because he loves his friends and they certainly showed their feelings for him. They brought cards, flowers, candy, games and Mike's spirits soared when he was with them. In turn, I truly believed he lifted everyone's spirits with his attitude. I know I always felt better when I was with him.

Chapter 2

Finding a New Way to Grow

Spending several weeks in the hospital, then in the rehabilitation center in Salt Lake City, gave me ample time to reflect on my life. How good it had been and how I had been fortunate to be raised by parents who really cared. I thought about a statement Og Mandino had written and how lucky I was to have been born to my folks. Og wrote, "How many parents, in moments of anger, push the 'kill' switch on one of their kids by telling their little boy or girl that he or she will never amount to anything? How many kids then spend a lifetime working very hard to make their parent's prophecy come true?"

I was born in the south-central rural Utah town of Fillmore, the second of seven children. My parents were the greatest friends and support system I could have hoped for. Because of our large family, and also because of our family's values, hard work and achieving personal potential were ingrained in my mind from as early as I could remember.

My brother, Scott, who is fifteen months my senior, was a special inspiration to me during my recovery. He had been part and parcel of my earliest memories ever since we moved to the small rural Utah town of Glenwood when I was just a year old.

My dad was the basketball coach of nearby Richfield High School and due to his influence, we grew up with a ball in our hands. It was the most natural way for us to spend our time. We also loved to fish and to play night games behind the nearby church. In whatever I did, the common thread of "competing" and being my very best was woven into my innermost fabric. It became me, and there was nothing I couldn't do. What's more, I seemed to have a natural talent for athletics and was always called out first to be on a team. Once chosen, it fell on my shoulders to lead out and direct whatever team I was on, and with my mind-set I relished the challenge.

During this time we had a hunting dog by the name of Skipper. He was an English Springer Spaniel. When he died we took his body over to Marshmallow Meadows, a place where we would roast marshmallows and there we had a private graveside service for him. It was sad and we were all crying, but I appreciated my dad's sensitivity to our needs, and my own sadness. Dad was right there getting us Skipper number two, however, so this helped us get over the loss of such a great companion.

My favorite recollection of this time was of going to the high school gym with Scott and my dad to play basketball. We were in seventh heaven when we did this, and nothing could be greater than a good game of basketball. I was a gym rat from day one and because I had a competitive bulldog nature, there wasn't anything I couldn't do with a ball in my hands.

Defining a Winner Mentality

When I was ten years old, I played on the Dodgers Little League baseball team and we won the city championship. This was the first time I thought of myself as a real "champion," and I'll never forget the feeling. I was the catcher and my big brother Scott, who was without question the best baseball player in the city, was the star pitcher. We were a duo that couldn't be denied, and I think that the love and mutual respect we have for each other, as adults, was actually put in place way back then. Having a competitive older brother can bring pleasures and perils. Such was the case with Scott and me. A year older than I, Scott was the model I always found myself trying to live up to, striving and stretching, extending myself beyond my limits. He was a great teacher, too, and took time to lift me to his level. Because of this, and because he included me in his activities, I will always have a special place in my heart for him. We had sibling rivalry, to be sure, but when things all boiled down, much of my progress, both as an athlete as well as a person, I owe to Scott.

The feeling of being "the best" accelerated even more when both of us made the All-Star baseball team. I wasn't the biggest or the best, by any means, but I was determined! More than any other thing, this determined mind-set was the thing that helped me adjust after the accident.

A few days following the accident, I was moved out of intensive care. Feeling somewhat better, I decided to pen my thoughts in the form of a poem. Because of its positive outlook, and since it clearly reflects my nearly fifteen-year-old mind-set, I have decided to share it as follows:

> *The things we've lost are the things that we love*
> *But if we live good lives, we will regain them above.*
> *Why things happen, God only knows*
> *But what is planned for us, time only shows.*
> *While we are waiting to find our spot,*
> *We need to start working with what we have got.*
>
> *We can take it easy or do the best we can,*
> *That shows the difference between a boy and a man.*
> *Where the path is rugged and the mountain steep,*
> *What we learn here is ours to keep.*
> *Where our vision stops is not the end,*
> *There is a whole new world just around the bend.*
>
> *So when there is nothing but troubles and everything's*
> *   wrong,*
> *Stiffen your mind and stand all the more strong.*
> *We were sent to this earth to take our test,*
> *So the Lord can find the good, the bad, and the best.*
> *If we live the gospel and keep on tryin'*
> *Before we know it, we will be in Zion.*

So, when all is lost, you've still got love
From your family, your friends, and your Father above.

The night after writing this poem, I received a surprise visit from my Grandma Schlappi. Having been moved to a different room in the hospital, I was feeling like I might even live. Anyway, she arrived late that night with a cherry Slurpee from 7-11. She said she was determined to give me an "unauthorized" treat. We visited, then she left just as a nurse came to take my temperature. I decided I'd have some fun, so after the nurse left, I took the thermometer out of my mouth and stuck it down into the last half of my Slurpee. Moments later, when I heard the nurse returning, I quickly put the thermometer back inside my mouth, then pretended to have dozed off.

Totally unsuspecting, she came into my room, extracted the thermometer, and read it. She then went hysterical, as she could see that I had died twenty or thirty degrees earlier! By this time, I couldn't contain myself and I burst out laughing. I thought it was the greatest joke ever. She didn't think so, however, and my antics ended up getting me in real trouble. It was worth it, though, since this was the first time I had laughed since the accident. It was at this moment that I realized something that has sustained me many times since. Although things didn't always go as I would have liked, still I could retain my sense of humor and keep life in perspective. That "laugh" was a real stepping-stone for me in the recovery process. From it I learned that I could still have fun, as any fifteen-year-old boy could, even though I would do it with wheelchair tires instead of gym shoes.

When I was finally transferred to the rehabilitation center, in Salt Lake City, I saw a patient scooting along the hallway, face down, on a cart. I could tell that he was blind, and I asked one of the attendants about him. He told me that the man, whose name was Bob, had been paralyzed in a car accident. As if that weren't enough, he quickly acquired a defeatist attitude. Sinking in despair, he finally put a gun in his mouth and pulled the trigger. The only problem was, he didn't kill himself. Instead, he instantly lost his eyesight, leaving him more disabled than ever.

So now Bob was both blind and in a wheelchair and with a much better attitude than he had before he shot himself. This illustrates the point that whether you have everything going for you or are totally disabled, the difference is measured by attitude.

I still had aches and pains, but I was convinced I would survive all of the healing and make a new life for myself. On a Wednesday I had a visitor I admired instantly because of the positive attitude he displayed. My mother's diary recorded the meeting between us:

About 9:00 P.M., Mike had a special visitor. Gifford Nielson, All-American quarterback from Brigham Young University, came to see him. He told Mike of his deep disappointment when he was favored to win the coveted Heiseman Trophy, then his hopes were dashed when he injured his knee. He counseled Mike to make his life a practice of looking forward and to keep a positive attitude. The remarkable thing that happened between the two of them was when Gifford leaned forward over the bottom of the bed to shake Mike's hand. Mike leaned forward from the top of the bed, but he could barely touch Gifford's fingertips. Gifford's stiff knee and Mike's handicap prevented contact. Mike smiled at his visitor and said, "Two handicaps don't work too well together." They both laughed.

Thursday: Mike had a good day today. He was sitting up at about a 75-degree angle. His friends called off and on during the day. That night we ordered a pizza and Grandpa and Grandma Palmer enjoyed it with him. Again, all the kids came over and Mike is trying to talk the doctors into letting him go to the Jr. High Harvest Festival. They did not feel it was the best thing for him. We visited with the Fetheroffs to find out if they had any insurance at all to help with our financial burden. Luckily, they did have a little and it helped.

Friday: Today was the day Mike was transferred to Holy Cross Hospital. Before leaving he was interviewed by Randy Riplinger, a KUTV news reporter, who wanted to do a special on Mike. He came into the hospital room and asked Mike what he was going to do in the future. Mike answered: "The same thing I would have done, but I'll do it differently."

After his transfer to Holy Cross, we stayed with Mike in his new room to make sure he was going to be okay. He had a roommate, a sixteen-year-old who had been hurt in a truck rollover. He was very quiet and withdrawn.

By Saturday the medics had stopped all of the pain shots and pills Mike had been taking. All of us were grateful that the pain in his back had subsided. But he was having problems with his eyes. His lids were heavy, ached, and his vision was blurred. When nurses tried to put him in a wheelchair he endured it for about fifteen minutes then got very dizzy.

The lift table which automatically elevated him up and down to send blood to his feet and head made him sick. The doctors told us that his reaction was common with injuries such as his.

By the following Tuesday when Grandma Palmer spent the day with Mike we thought the turning point had come because he was feeling stronger and more stable. Harry James, University of Utah's tennis coach — who was also paralyzed — brought a tennis player with him and the three visited. James gave Mike some hand controls for his car to use when he could drive again. He also told Mike that everyone has some kind of handicap. 'You just can't see the ones others have,' he explained. He invited Mike to come and watch the U of U team work out. He promised that he would help him learn more about wheelchair tennis.

On the Friday after Thanksgiving Mike had a big workout day. The rehabilitation instructor had him climb into his chair by himself and he lifted weights in the physical therapy room.

When Saturday came and Mike's dad and I got to the hospital, he was popping "wheelies" in his wheelchair.

Monday rolled around and we learned that Mike had been having pains all day in his stomach and shoulder. X-rays had been taken and the doctors suspected one of three things: an ulcer, pulled muscles or a blood clot. Of course, we were alarmed and anxious to know exactly what was happening. The doctors said they would run more tests and x-rays the next day. Mike's new symptoms were not supposed to happen. He had been feeling so good. The diagnosis of a blood clot in his system was confirmed.

I met Mike's new roommate whose name is "Bert." He is about 27 and six feet tall. He was in an industrial accident two months earlier and suffered brain damage. The medics operated and were giving him a better chance of recovery with marked improvement every day. He made Mike laugh so hard. Though his reactions and reflexes were very slow, he always came up with a witty answer in his slow monotone voice.

Mike played wheelchair basketball with him and the two of them laughed themselves silly. Mike was sure he would never forget that game.

———

Needless to say, I did recover from the blood clot. It dissipated and went away and the day for my discharge from the hospital grew closer.

Chapter 3

Attitude Therapy

As you've learned in the preceding pages, I received a lot of physical and occupational therapy following my accident and I was plenty grateful for it, believe me. Even so, my greatest therapy was the therapy I gave to myself. I called it Attitude Therapy. It is not about trying to change a situation we don't like. Rather it is about changing our attitude and perspective toward the situation. This notion of Attitude Therapy evolved in me and is now the name of my speaking business. I've often heard it said that "Our attitude determines our altitude," and I believe it. Regardless of how much help I received from those attending me, I knew intuitively that the greatest therapy was in my mind-and consisted of what I convinced myself to do and to become. I knew that I would have physical limitations, but I also knew that within these limitations I could achieve anything I determined to achieve. From where I sat, there was no holding back and I began to relish the challenge of each new day!

I made up my mind that I would overcome the hurdle of my crippled legs and find a different way to travel. Before I left the hospital, I was awarded patient of the month for my positive attitude and my good influence on the staff and patients in the rehabilitation division. My parents were warned by the social workers that I would come home and be very frustrated and go through screaming fits, periods of extreme depression and black moods. I never did and I believe it is because I took responsibility for my situation and gave myself heavy doses of attitude therapy each and every day. Sometimes it was just memorizing a poem. Other times it was closing my eyes and counting my blessings. Still other times it was just accepting that even though my legs would atrophy, I could still love myself from the inside out. I like to say that the average person spends 45–50 minutes each and every day looking good for the world on the outside. Things like combing our hair or putting on our makeup. We should spend just as much time giving ourselves pep talks or attitude therapy each day.

Harvard Medical School each years holds a conference called *Spirituality in Healing*. Attendees learn that the mind, body, and spirit are very much connected. In a sense, through attitude therapy we can be our own doctor or therapist. Over time, if people work at it, they realize that they can begin to "train the brain" how to think and respond in a more positive way. You begin to look at other people or your own situations and you find the positive aspects. I know you can't just tell someone to have a good attitude and presto it is done, like magic. It is a skill that has to be learned and developed. It takes time and practice. It takes someone who can count blessings as easily as problems. I used a lot of humor when I was first injured. I remember thinking things like, geez, my legs look like I went on a diet from the waist down.

Humor was a coping mechanism for me. We are really like computers. What we put into our minds and spirits and hearts is all that can come out. So we must put in the good before the good can come out. I had so many positive experiences and such great family and friend support that I could draw on. My tank had reserve fuel and I was not on empty. My accident didn't push me completely over the edge when the thought of suicide would pop into my mind. I would not be truthful, however, if I didn't admit that there were times when I would have liked to close my eyes and end it all.

Another aspect of attitude therapy is taking life one day at a time. I was always a goal setter before my accident. I thought of the future and doing great things like playing college basketball or being the student body president of the college I attended.

Following my accident, I wasn't sure what the next day would bring. I couldn't worry about the future and go back to school until

I could get dressed. I couldn't drive a car until I could transfer into the car. I couldn't like a girl until I liked myself. My goals therefore, became simple things like popping a wheelie and jumping up a curb in my chair. Before my accident, I never thought twice about stepping up on a curb, but now it seemed like such a big obstacle in a chair. I learned that all of these small successes were essential before I could refocus on my larger lifetime dreams. I just had to step back before I could move forward. The principles in my new life actually began to take shape in the hospital. I thought about my new situation as a challenge to overcome — an opponent to win over. When I saw someone else in my situation in the rehab hospital who was about ready to go home, I told myself if he can do it, so can I.

Looking back, this thing I called attitude therapy didn't stop me from having a bad day, but I think it stopped me from having bad weeks and months. I know a 15-year-old doesn't always think too deeply, but I believe these concepts can be applied by any parent, businessman, salesperson, spouse, athlete, elderly person, or anyone who tends to first see the negative aspects of life, instead of praising the positive ones.

When I returned home from the hospital, I was prepared for some serious sympathy. What I didn't know, of course, was that my parents had discussed my situation at length, and had determined to treat me no differently than they had before.

Dad was more of a pusher than Mom, and she was more the unconditional loving and compassionate mother. Both parents were supportive, of course, but Mom was especially helpful encouraging me to regain my self-worth, an identity that, previous to my being shot, had revolved around the strength and coordination of my hands and legs.

I knew my father was often frustrated and even angry toward my friend, Torrey. This was understandable because of the high hopes he had had for me as an athlete. As time went by, however, he accepted the situation and planted seeds of promise in my mind that I could still be a great athlete.

My jobs around the house were still the same, and with the family garden this meant that I had to wheel myself along between the rows of vegetables, weeding by hand with no excuses. I wasn't exactly excited about this chore, but their wisdom eliminated any possibility of pity parties, and I moved ahead thinking of myself as normal — no disability.

Another chore that remains vivid in my memory was the daily routine of setting the table before a meal, then washing the dishes afterward. I learned to stack the used dishes in my lap, take them from the dining room to the kitchen, then sit sideways against the sink and rinse them off before putting them in the dishwasher.

My folks were smart enough to let me figure out the "hows" for myself. They supplied the "what" and there was really no discussion afterward. So, with their approach to my disablement, I soon learned to cope with my responsibilities — to do things like my siblings did them even though I was in a wheelchair.

In the long run, I was a much better person for the way I was treated. I don't mean to infer that my folks didn't find things for me to do that were more suitable to my condition. In fact, whether it was fixing a sprinkler head that had broken, or the necessity for me to vacuum the part of the house where I lived, there was plenty for me to do. Being limited, I was forced to think ahead, to anticipate my needs. I'm sure this forward-looking way of doing things has spilled into all areas of my life.

One of my greatest blessings at this time was my sister, Julie. She was three years younger than I, but even so, she grew up in a hurry following my accident, and quite literally became my own private nurse. There was nothing she wouldn't do for me, and even though we had very normal brother/sister squabbles, we also grew very close.

My other siblings helped as well, and with their support and encouragement, I soon found myself rekindling the same attitude of success that had sustained me thus far in my life. Deep inside, I knew the power of my mind and within limitations there wasn't anything I couldn't do. For me, it was the perfect place to begin my long road back.

Choosing the "Right" Friends

When I graduated from elementary school and moved on into junior high, I attended Lakeridge Junior High School. When I entered my very first classroom, Arts and Crafts, I met Roger, whom I mentioned earlier. I sat down and looked around, and eyeballing him, I said, "Hi, my name's Mike." "I'm Roger," he replied, "Roger Dayton." We shook hands, cementing the beginning of a friendship that has continued to this day. He and his parents, Gary and Zona, were especially supportive of me after my accident and I owe them a great deal.

There wasn't anything Roger wouldn't do for me, nor me for him. Not only that, but I always knew where he stood on things. I knew he had values and standards, and that being with him would motivate me to stand for the same things.

My other closest childhood friend was Doug Jensen, who went with me to college. While Doug was a good athlete, especially as a tennis player, this sport didn't consume his life. Together we would hang out, play chess or table tennis, or just chase around with high school and college buddies.

Other friends were of Roger and Doug's same quality. What I appreciated more than anything was the fact that these associates still wanted to be my friends! This realization came slowly, and sank deep into my heart. Other than my family, these friends were my cheerleaders and they loved me for who I was on the inside, rather than being stymied by my outward limitations. Often, at lunch, my friends and I would leave school. We'd throw my chair in the trunk of whoever's car we were driving and we'd head to McDonalds. I remember one time these friends jumped out of the car and began ordering their Big Macs, without realizing that I was still in the car. This experience actually made me feel good, knowing that my friends thought of me as "normal," and not too consumed with my chair.

Personal Lesson

I would now like to share an experience that happened to me about a year after my accident. It was responsible for another shift in my attitude about life.

When I turned sixteen, about a year after the accident, one rite of passage that seemed pretty important to me was to purchase my first deer hunting license, then go hunting with my dad and brother. I'd legally hunted pheasants since I was twelve, so the yearly fall ritual was deep inside me. Even though I would be hunting deer from a sitting position against a tree, and would not be able to stomp through the trees and brush as before, the effort would be well worth it.

The opening morning of deer hunting season finally arrived, and before I knew it my arms and legs were wrapped around Dad on his horse and we were moving up the slopes in the mountain range east of Fillmore, Utah. When we finally decided on a good spot for me to position myself, I was lifted off the horse, propped up against a large pine, and handed my rifle.

Dad and the others then moved on with the objective of working below me to stir a deer up through the trees for me to shoot.

I had not been there long when a herd of thirteen or fourteen elk came along, not even noticing me. I watched them, totally enthralled with their beauty and majesty. If I were to be totally truthful, I was scared to death. I could just see them trampling on me with no way to save myself. After they left, I heard other noises, probably deer, over the ridge; but in my mind I could just see a bear coming toward me. My mind really began playing tricks, and I had a hard time settling down.

Not long after this, a nice two-point buck came into the clearing below. I was ready for him, and swung my rifle to my shoulder, pulled the trigger, and dropped the buck with one shot. It was a nice first time trophy, and I couldn't have been more proud. After years of hunting with my dad, and carrying our lunch, I had finally bagged my very own deer.

Not long after I shot the buck, another hunter came along, the deer jumped up on his front legs and began dragging himself along with his broken back, trying to escape. The hunter shot it again, and this time it stayed down. It was just about fifty yards from me.

I yelled, "Hey, dude!" and the man came over to me on his horse. As calmly as possible, I explained that I had already shot the deer. Seeing my plight, he was pretty cool about it, and asked if he could gut it for me. He could see that I was paralyzed and was not going anywhere. He calmly went out of his way to help. I thanked him, and before I knew it he had dragged the deer over to a nearby tree, cleaned and dressed it, and left it hanging to cool off. I thanked him sincerely, and he was once again on his way.

Later in the day, when my dad and the others returned, several of them had likewise bagged their bucks. Were they ever surprised, though, to see that not only had I killed my first deer, but it was dressed and ready to carry out. They wasted no time, and soon both the deer and I were hoisted up onto the horse, and we were headed back to camp.

Earlier, when I saw that my deer hadn't died with my shot, I suddenly had a surge of empathy and sadness that I had never before known. The deer was no different than myself, I thought. I knew what it was experiencing — the pain, the sense of hopelessness, the broken back, the loss. What's more, I didn't have a wheelchair to offer the deer, nor a pain-killer to lessen his pain.

I suddenly felt differently about killing than ever before. I knew the Lord had provided for our family to have an increase of meat for the winter and I'd had a great time, but somehow I valued life, and the deer's loss of his more deeply and in an entirely different way.

I'm not sure of all that happened to me on that deer hunt, but from that day on I began to take life a little more seriously. In fact, since then I've never killed a deer. I have been satisfied to shoot them with my camera.

You Think Having a Bad Hair Day Is Bad

Not long after my first hunting trip, I went with my family and my friend, Roger Dayton, to Deer Creek Reservoir. We spent the day water-skiing, although I was confined to the boat. I hadn't yet learned to water-ski, but I had learned to have fun.

After all the others had finished skiing, it was suddenly my turn. So I put on a life jacket and flipped over the edge of the boat into the water. Perhaps I should mention that at this time there were no special water skis for the disabled. All we had was a round yellow plywood board that my friend, Roger, had brought along. So I pulled myself onto this board, grabbed hold of the rope, and signaled for my dad to open up the throttle.

We took off at full speed and I hung on for dear life. I can't say that I wasn't frightened, because I was. Still, even though the water was hitting me in the face and making it hard to see, it was then that I noticed the people in our boat laughing. I thought that perhaps one of my sisters, Julie or Collette, had told a joke; but I remembered that neither of them were very funny.

Then, almost immediately Dad swung the boat around and headed for shore. By this time, I was becoming self-conscious. I looked over my shoulder and saw that my legs were flapping around in the breeze, giving everyone a good laugh. I thought that maybe I looked like a flying frog as I was skipping along the water, having a good time.

But there was a worse problem. I glanced behind me and was horrified to learn that the water had pushed my swimsuit completely off my atrophied legs! I was literally skiing in my birthday suit! Well, my brain wasn't paralyzed, so I quickly slid off the board and let go of the rope. I then waited for Dad to circle around in the boat and pick me up.

I was mortified, but while I bobbed up and down in the water, I suddenly realized that this moment was much like my accident. I couldn't help what had happened to me, but my attitude could determine how I responded to it. I could either laugh at myself, and enjoy the humor of the moment, or I could sulk and get upset with how the others were acting. It was a great wake-up call for me, and a memory that had much to do with my future.

Somehow I regained my dignity, borrowed an extra pair of shorts from my sister, then got back in the boat. We had a good time laughing and joking as I told everyone I was the world's first nude disabled water-skier. Let me add something profound. I experienced firsthand that having a "bad butt day" is worse than having a "bad hair day!"

On a subsequent trip to the same reservoir, I had an even greater tragedy, but with very severe consequences. We were driving down the canyon after water-skiing with Roger Dayton in his very old truck. Although I was unaware of it, the truck floorboard had a predictable habit of becoming very, very hot, and with no feeling in my feet, and with nothing covering them for protection, I was oblivious to any problem until I began smelling barbecued meat. What I didn't know was that I was the barbecue, with my feet being burned all the way through to the bone. The only good thing about this was that I had no pain. The bad thing was that I wasn't able to wear shoes for about six months after that.

The point of sharing this story is that the perils and consequences of being paralyzed are many, and often unpredictable and unanticipated. I now had to be more alert than ever before. Either that, or I would spend my life banged or burned up.

Cheer Up, Things Could Be Worse!

Well, I cheered up, and sure enough ... things definitely got worse!

Several months after my accident, I found myself in an arm wrestling competition with Coach Fuller, my weight-lifting coach at Orem High School. We were in his social studies classroom, and my girlfriend at the time was watching us. We went all out, and before I knew it, he had won, breaking my arm and leaving me racked with pain. My funny bone was broken, and was pulled all the way up to my wrist. However, I found it anything but funny! I thus spent the next two months with a cast extending from my wrist to my shoulder.

Not only was this injury very painful, but it greatly limited my ability to get around. Although I hate to admit it, I went "in circles" for these two months, getting nowhere. Just kidding. Truly, I was slowed down, but this interruption in my progress caused me to learn entirely new dimensions about patience, as well as being recipient of the "law of the harvest." I showed off and became stubborn, and I paid big time for it. During this visit to the hospital, the doctor turned me over and surgically removed the bullet from my back. Prior to this it had felt like an extra vertebrae in my spine.

I held this little piece of lead in the palm of my hand and thought about all the pain and damage it had caused.

I also realized that it had taken me to places in my life that I never would have gone otherwise. I can honestly say that this is about the time I accepted my situation. I was glad to finally have it out of my system — in more ways than one.

I also had a hard time dealing with the phantom pains in my legs, the bathroom complexities, and so forth. I soon learned that although this was reality, I was no different than anyone else. Just because others don't have a wheelchair strapped to their back, that doesn't mean they don't have their adversities. Life is a challenge, and must be faced with courage and resolve.

Still, even with an overall positive attitude, I had my moments of near discouragement and despair. One of these moments occurred not long after I got out of the hospital. I was back in school and one afternoon my buddies and I went to the sophomore basketball game. Two friends carried me up into the bleachers and as the game unfolded, I could hardly watch. Instead, I quietly wept, feeling sorry for myself and despairing over the fact that I would never again play basketball on my feet with my brother, Scott. It was a dark hour for me, one that I still remember as though it were yesterday.

About three years after the accident, my mom bought me a record by Barry Manilow. The name of one of the songs on this album was, *I Made It Through the Rain.* It was a beautiful song, and since she thought I had progressed through the worst of things, she sensed it would be a comfort to me. It was, too, and I appreciated her sensitivity. I was on an unexpected learning curve with one storm after another, but I was amazed at how far I had come in a short time.

In the years since I was paralyzed, my life has become a demonstration of the power God gives to each one of us to make a personal triumph of our lives. The energy in the promise I made to Him when I prayed for my life after I was shot, allowed me to become a two-time Paralympic gold medal winner and the only wheelchair basketball player to compete and earn medals in four consecutive Paralympic Games, in Seoul, Barcelona,

Atlanta and Sydney. I have been honored in my home state of Utah as one of its Top 50 Athletes of the Twentieth Century, and I've served on the Board of Trustees for the 2002 Olympic Games in Salt Lake City.

But success means more to me than to be honored at the White House, or admired by audiences around the world I address on the unconquerable power of the human spirit to rise above adversity. It means that when you believe in God you become a missionary for the true purpose of life: To become your own star, to chart a direction by which you can magnify your soul, as a reflection of the magnificence of God you discover in yourself.

Paradigms of Purpose

It has been said that the best predictor of future behavior is past behavior. I knew that if I was going to get back to my productive, success-oriented self, I would need to grow up in a hurry and face life straight on. This meant that I would have to think in a much more mature manner and that I could not return to my adolescent carefree mentality.

Don Hutson, in his book *The Sale,* stressed the point that looking back is a useless emotion with no intrinsic value. If we could put ourselves (or even others) into some kind of rewind mode, or if we could relive an event, it might be useful. But we can't do this, so we shouldn't burn up energy looking backward. Instead, we should learn from the past, then look forward with "an eye of hope."

Returning to my observable improvement, as I continued to take stock of my life, I came to several life-altering shifts in my mind-set. That is, I began to view life in a different way — seeing things from a different perspective and with a much clearer lens and focus. These life views are called paradigms, or expectations. They followed what could have been a tragedy for me, and have built upon each other in these sequential steps:

Paradigm One: Small successes, if repeated, lead to large successes. For me, this began with simply being able to partially dress myself. Now, years later, caring for my personal needs is relatively easy and automatic. While I have to often become creative in how I accomplish things there is nothing I can't do. It's a great way to live life. Confidence is born of small successes, and having an increase in ability makes it all worthwhile in the end.

Paradigm Two: Passions don't die simply because we are injured, physically or emotionally. For me, this meant that I decided to pursue life with the same enthusiasm I had prior to my accident. After all, my spirit wasn't paralyzed and I could still soar with the other eagles! Akin to this idea is that we should focus on what we have left, rather than on what we may have lost. Having this mind-set has helped me want not to quit, want not to become a disabled victim, and want not to ultimately become a burden to society.

I love the sentence I heard somewhere that "All motivation is self-motivation." It's true and one of the most inspirational examples of this concept was recently reported in a newspaper in an article by Ed Heroldsen. He described a senior citizen named Thora DeWolf, who drove alone to her second home in Nauvoo, Illinois. Four days after her arrival, she fell and broke both shoulders which left her helpless and alone for five long days. Unable to eat or drink, and to even move, this courageous woman maintained hope that she wouldn't die there. On the fifth day, Thora was able to turn over on her back. This allowed her to call out loud enough to be heard by a neighbor taking a stroll.

Thora was rescued, then flown to a hospital in nearby Keokuk, Iowa. After several weeks in the hospital where she was not only bedridden, but was unable to feed and care for herself she gradually began physical therapy. This consisted of moving her hands in small circles several times a day. This ability led to another, and before long she was not only out of the rehab center, but was doing community service on a full-time basis.

Reflecting on her recovery experience, Thora said, "When I first started to exercise it was painful and I was overcome at the end of the day. But the next morning I would feel so wonderful! I got the message that if I ever wanted to be normal again, I had to do it because no one else could do this for me."

Talk about one who is in charge of her life! Perhaps the most remarkable aspect of Thora's experience is her age. She is eighty-two years young, and still waking each day to serve, living her passion in every way!

Paradigm Three: Regardless of our limitations we don't need to consider ourselves "handicapped." For me, this meant that I teach myself to not use my wheelchair as a *crutch!* This is not to say that I didn't have to be on guard, for just the opposite was true. Still, even though I could barbeque my feet, or lose my shorts in a very unique manner, I was no different from anyone else. I had my challenges, but so does everyone.

We all have challenges, whether they're obvious like mine, or more hidden, such as the emotional trauma of a death or divorce. In a recent lecture given in Salt Lake City, noted psychologist Dr. Page Bailey taught that injury is an interruption of expectations. Everyone at some time or another experiences injury. It is then up to that person to create new expectations, and to not allow his or her misfortune to derail expectations and leave his or her pain and anguish as unhappy memories.

Regardless of my injury, I determined to never consider myself handicapped. My expectations had been interrupted, but only for a short time. I soon learned to expect as much from myself as before the accident, maybe even more. This is why I have used the word "disabled" throughout this book, rather than the word handicapped.

Paradigm Four: We should not blame others when "bad" things happen. In other words, we should be responsible for ourselves. I first learned this lesson when I was about seven years old. One day, while visiting my folks' bedroom, I noticed a red cherry-looking ball on the top of their dresser. It had what looked like a fuse on it, so I stuffed it into my pocket and left the room. Devising a very complex plan, I found some matches, retreated to the back yard under a willow tree, and set the fuse on fire.

Jumping back, I was fortunate not to be injured when the "cherry bomb" blew! The entire neighborhood heard the noise and my goose was cooked in one inescapable instant. Not only that, but the bomb had blown a foot-wide hole in the grass, and when my folks learned what I'd done, I was in the doghouse. I had to take responsibility for what I'd done, and so I did, although for the life of me I can't recall the punishment I received.

By the same token, when I reflected on my shooting accident, I honestly didn't blame my friend for what happened to me. I was in his parents' bedroom, I was handling his dad's pistol, and just because he pulled the trigger and accidentally shot me, didn't make him solely responsible for what happened. We were in it together and while I became the initial victim, the subsequent blessings in my life far outweigh the limitations. In fact, because of this accident, I may have even accomplished more than I would have if I had been able to continue employing the use of my legs!

Girls, Girls, and More Girls!

Shifting gears, part of my maturing response to life [and therefore my attitude] included feelings for and experiences with the opposite sex. While I wasn't the greatest catch in our high school, somehow I didn't know that and after turning sixteen, I began to date with great regularity. I not only had an electrifying handshake, but I also did wheelies in my chair, and in general "did my thing" with the young ladies. Now, to be truthful, I haven't met very many girls who made it a practice to follow handicapped license plates home and who preferred dating wheelchair-bound guys. Even so, I decided early on that I would not accept pity, nor would I view myself as being disabled, per se. Rather, I was just a guy who had to dance in my wheelchair.

This realization didn't come easy. In fact, I really hesitated to ask a girl to dance with someone who couldn't dance. Then something fortuitous took place. I went to one particular dance, and before long a girl by the name of Wendy invited me onto the floor. I was pretty slow in rolling on out, but before long I was doing the wheelies I mentioned earlier, twisting around, and goofing off until the song ended. Thanking her for asking me, I was about to turn and head back to my safe corner. After all, I didn't even want to be at the dance, let alone on the dance floor.

Wendy then caught me completely off-guard by inviting me to dance the next song, a slow one, no less! I was stuck, and I knew it, so waiting to see what her next move would be, I just sat there, as if I had any choice! Neither of us knew what to do at that point, so she approached me, then got down on her knees next to my chair. Now the pressure was on me, and [pardon the pun] I was sweating bullets! Not knowing I had better options, I started patting her on the head to the beat of the music. Before long, however, I invited her to sit on my lap so we could coast around in each other's arms. My mom hadn't raised any dummies, I assure you, and suddenly I was floating on clouds, realizing yet another advantage to being wheelchair bound!

That initial slow dance with Wendy led to others on other evenings and gave me a chance to have my dates sit on my lap both while dancing a slow dance and at picture-taking time. Their perfume was intoxicating and keeping socially active was as therapeutic as any other aspect of my teen life. What's more, as my wheelchair antics became known, my buddies started taking my extra wheelchairs to dances, just to have their dates sit in their laps. Those wheelchairs really were in vogue, and provided us all with great moments of closeness with the girls!

Caught Without a Chair

Sometime later, as I accelerated my activities as a normal teenager, Halloween rolled around. Not one to stay home and hand out treats, the night arrived with several buddies and I chasing around in one of their cars, seeing what evil deeds we could accomplish. I was sitting in the middle of the back seat, flanked by two friends. We were chucking tomatoes and water balloons at the trick-or-treaters, scaring them and in general having a lot of fun. I had left my wheelchair at home, however, because there wasn't room for it, with our balloons and the tomatoes.

Unfortunately, the local police caught on to our pranks, and pulled us over. They ordered all of us out of the car, and my buddies quickly responded. But, as you'd guess, I could do nothing but sit there. When one of the cops challenged me, I told him I couldn't get out because I was in a wheelchair.

"Where's your chair?" he challenged, thinking he had me dead-to-rights in a lie.

"Uh … I left it home."

"Sure you did. And tonight's not Halloween, either!"

Thinking I was being a smart alec, the policeman then grabbed me by the shoulder and pulled me out of the car. I complied, of course, but with disastrous consequences. As I came out the back door, I fell hard against the road. Shocked into the reality of my disabled state, the cop helped me back up into the car, totally tongue-tied. I'm sure that's an experience he'll never forget. I won't either, since I had to do several hours of community service!

Reflecting on these early experiences, I have thought of how our society has labeled people, whether they have too many zits, can't dance slow dances, carry an extra fifty pounds, don't wear designer clothes, or even get confronted by a cop who thought I was someone I was not on Halloween night. We've been conditioned to be picky and judgmental about non-relevant issues, creating stereotypes that really limit our vision about people. I've found that the happiest, most enjoyable people to be around are those who look for the good in others, then are blind to whatever "deficiencies" they might have. After all, we all have deficiencies, and that's called LIFE!

Attitude Therapy Summarized

Charles Swindoll, in speaking about attitude, said something that deserves restating:

"The longer I live, the more I realize the impact one's attitude has on life. Attitude, to me, is more important than facts. It is more important than the past, than education, than money, than circumstance, than failures, than successes, than what other people think or say or do. It is more important than appearance, giftedness or skill. What's more, it will make or break a company, a church, a home and of course, a person.

"The remarkable thing is we have a choice every day regarding the attitude we will embrace for that day. We cannot change our past, we cannot change the fact that people will act in a certain way. We cannot change the inevitable. The only thing we can do is play on the one string we have, and that is our attitude.

"I am convinced that life is ten percent what happens to me, and ninety percent how I react to it. And so it is with you. We are in charge of our attitudes!"

Adding to this, Dallin H. Oaks, a noted Supreme Court judge, once said that three ingredients comprise the inner man. These include (1) our motives, (2) our desires, and (3) our attitude. He went on to observe that "Motives explain actions completed. Desires identify actions contemplated. Attitudes are the thought processes by which we evaluate our actions and experiences. Motives, desires, and attitudes are interdependent."

As I have attempted to articulate, Attitude Therapy is the therapy we give to ourselves. It is not occupational or physical therapy; nor is it speech therapy or recreational therapy. Rather, it is seeking to recover "from the inside out." This is the magic of attitude therapy. If we can incorporate this self-therapy without receiving our doctor's degree, then it means we should consider it. After all, from time to time each of us needs to sculpt, change, or reframe the way we think.

Chapter 4

Reaching Out —
The Magic of Serving

Before speaking of how I have grown through serving, which, by the way, I now believe is the main ingredient to having a happy life, I would like to examine this orientation from another perspective. Following my accident, I struggled with accepting help from anyone. I just wanted to "do it myself." What I soon learned, however, is that when I allowed people to help me, and serve my needs, they were growing and feeling better about themselves than ever before. It's much easier to give than to receive, at least for me. The following words have become my motto:"*If your lot in life feels empty, build a service station.*" The idea of letting others do things for me did not come easy. Gradually, however, I became aware of how crucial gracious receiving is, both for the giver, as well as for the receiver. It helps everyone!

And now the other side of the coin.

Although I try to keep my weaknesses pretty much to myself, I haven't always made a conscious effort to think of others. In fact, when I was a little boy, I thought the world sort of revolved around me. Not only was I gifted athletically, but I was also quite quick, mentally. I always prided myself in learning my times tables ahead of the class, impressing my teachers, and so forth.

One time, however, when I was in the third grade, I had an experience that jarred me out of my self-serving moorings. I misbehaved in class, although I don't really remember what I did wrong, and my teacher, Mrs. Warner, grabbed me by the ear and escorted me to the principal's office. It was a sobering moment, for sure, and a dose of humility that I must have needed at that juncture of my life.

One of the ideas that came to me early, probably when I was heading into the sixth grade at Westmore Elementary School, was that I wanted to be student body president of every school I attended. This dream became a reality, as I was elected president of my elementary school my final year there. That experience did as much for me as athletics did, and when I entered junior high and high school, I was elected to the same office.

The other experience I had early in my life that caused me to reach beyond myself was getting involved in Cub Scouts as well as the Boy Scouts. I earned the two highest honors in these programs, Arrow of Light, in Cub Scouts, and the rank of Eagle, in Boy Scouts. I never once thought that I couldn't achieve these ranks and in doing so I began to consider the needs and feelings of others. Also, I learned that you can make more friends in two weeks by becoming interested in other people than you can in two years by trying to get other people interested in you.

Both of the scouting programs were service oriented and I especially appreciated my Eagle Service Project. For this, I organized a program that would enable elementary-age children to safely walk the mile from school to the local church youth meetings on Wednesday afternoons. A lot of construction was going on in the area, so their safety was a crucial problem. I organized and enlisted adult crossing guard volunteers, as well as a system that ensured safe passage for these kids. I supervised this program for the two months of construction on the roads, and when it was over, I felt like I had really helped out.

Still, with all this service mentality, following my accident I honestly thought that I had lost the ability to serve. I no longer had use of my legs and somehow I equated legs with service. I would see my buddies helping move a family in or out of their home and I wanted to help, too. But I couldn't. Instead, I stayed home, feeling limited in my capacity to give.

Oatmeal Cereal

One morning, several years later when I was living in California, I decided to cook oatmeal cereal for breakfast. I had the water boiling, and was pouring the flakes into the pan when I unknowingly spilled some of the oatmeal flakes onto my lap. I was all spiffied up in a suit and tie, ready for a successful day. Immediately, I went out the front door to brush the flakes off my lap. Sitting in my wheelchair, I let my front wheels down off the curb to make it easier for the flakes to fall off my lap and into the gutter.

I lost my balance and tumbled out of the chair and into the gutter. My wheelchair also tipped over next to me, and I looked terrible and felt even worse. My next thought was, well, I'll just pull myself upright, straighten my chair, then climb back into it hoping no one would notice. As luck would have it, however, at that very instant a black Trans Am sports car rounded the corner and headed up the street toward me. Hoping the driver wouldn't see me, I tried to hide behind my wheelchair in the gutter. This ploy didn't work, however, as the driver behind the wheel not only noticed me, but stopped.

A young lady on the passenger side, rolled down her window and called out, "Sir, may we help you?"

"No, thanks," I quipped, trying to be funny. "I'm just having breakfast."

Feeling uncomfortable, the girl rolled up her window, and the car sped away.

As I made my way back into my chair and into the house, I felt badly for two reasons: First, I had not allowed someone the opportunity to serve me when she wanted to and second, she may never again offer her assistance to a person in need. I had really blown it!

Since then, whenever I'm asked by someone how he can help a disabled person, I say, do the kind of thing this young lady did — just ask. This not only opens the door for assistance, but allows the recipient to say "yes," or "no," depending on his or her own needs and perspective. I believe courtesy is always in fashion, whether directed toward someone who is disabled, or simply in need. If the recipient does not appreciate your courtesy, then perhaps the problem lies with him. Still, you can feel good about offering. Rather than ignoring an opportunity to serve, I always say, "When in doubt, help people out."

In an incident similar to this, I was leaving a shopping mall one day when I noticed a lady next to me in a business suit, who was walking toward the same exit. When we were both about thirty feet from the door, I wondered whether or not I should open the door for this business woman. I'm sure she had the same thought about helping me. Without waiting for her to speak, I looked at her and said, "I'll get the door for you this time, and you can get it for me next time." She thanked me, and we were both comfortable in leaving the mall.

From this incident, as well as many others, my thinking gradually evolved and I realized I could serve every bit as well from a wheelchair as I could from a standing position. I would simply focus on my strengths, and help people however and whenever I could. In fact, my favorite type of service, that which produces the most profound sense of fulfillment in my heart, is visiting newly injured individuals at hospitals and rehab centers. I am able to give them hope as well as an example of what is possible to achieve if they don't give up. Finally [this time with a pun intended] I am a roll model! Because of my condition, the disabled are able to relate with me in a more natural way than they can relate to those attending them. There is instant rapport, and empathy going both ways and each of us is made better by the exchange.

I'm sure this process of helping people re-frame their condition gave momentum for me to begin public speaking. Even today, when I need to spend more time with my family, it is difficult for me to turn down an opportunity to speak, especially to a group of young people. They need all the help they can get, so I try to meet their needs whenever possible.

I have learned a motto which I recommend to everybody:

> *Do all the good you can*
> *By all the means you can*
> *In all the ways you can*

At all the times you can
In all the places you can
To everyone you can.

My "Havenly" Home

When I think of the home I grew up in, in Orem, Utah, I think of the house, itself, as well as my family. Both were all a guy could ask for. Our home was located on a half acre of beautiful orchard land, with a massive garden. I'll have to admit that I liked the orchards better than the garden, simply because of the weeding and tending the garden required. I had my very own row to hoe and it was like a rain cloud that hung over me all the time. There were always more weeds to pull, and because I was the kind of kid to get my jobs done before playing, I never really got hassled. Of course, that's my memory and I'll stick to it.

But the orchards, well … they were the stuff life was made of for a growing boy. I owned a pellet gun and a BB gun, and I would wander through the orchards, shooting birds and fashioning myself into an out-and-out sharpshooter. I would envision the pheasant hunts and using my shotgun and these fantasies put me in a world of its own. One time, when a bird flew overhead, I cocked my BB gun, aimed, and fired. Believe it or not, I shot the bird while it was in flight. I didn't think about any moral issues in killing birds, since it was legal to do so, but I sure did consider myself an expert marksman.

Our home was a split-level type, and with such a large family it was not underutilized by any means. My brother, Scott, and I shared a bedroom and bathroom and even a queen-size bed. We'd get upset with each other at night whenever we crossed over our imaginary "side" of the bed, but we didn't get angry enough to stop being friends.

My First Real Jobs

Because I wanted money to do things with, and since Mom and Dad wanted us kids to learn to take responsibility, we contracted to manage a paper route. Not only did I have my own route to deliver each morning, but we had to get up at 3:30 A.M. and deliver the bundles of papers to the other carriers for their routes. I can honestly say that I hated doing this, although I for sure didn't hate getting the monthly check in the mail.

The other early-on job I had was selling donuts. I would make a few cents a dozen, but I never did have much money from it. Instead, I'd earn some money, then turn around and buy a dozen for myself and my friends. My profits always seemed to be "eaten up," leaving me only with the holes!

These early habits of working were profitable in the long run, as I would save a percentage of what I earned. This money went into an account for college, and came in quite handy when I finally reached that age of tuition needs.

I also got a job at a nearby restaurant. I didn't wait on tables, of course, but kept the salad bar. I would re-stock it, clean it up, and in general hover over it so that the restaurant's patrons would think it was the "best in town." I enjoyed working there, too, and feeling that there was something productive I could still do. It was great therapy for me.

It was while working there and experiencing back pain that I made the decision to spend my life supporting my family through the use of my brain, rather than through my upper torso brawn. Adding fuel to this decision was another job I had and that was teaching first and second graders how to read. They would be assigned to come to our house for lessons and I would help them develop their reading skills. Looking back, I'm sure this early exposure to instructing helped me every bit as much as it helped them. From what I've experienced, teaching is the most rewarding profession there is.

Still, I don't want to paint a picture of all work, for it was not that way. My brother and I would always be building a fort out in the orchard; and we would sit there and tell stories by the hour. We'd also sneak food out of the house, especially graham crackers or cookies and stock the fort with whatever food we could get. We'd also take off for the sandpits and hunt lizards, catching them whenever we could. Two brothers couldn't have been more caught up with just being boys.

Family Traditions

It was Thomas Carlyle who defined the value of tradition when he wrote: "What an enormous magnifier is tradition!" And this was the quality in our family which I learned to appreciate and feel part of.

"Home" was, of course, my family. With seven children to care for, there were always plenty of chores for each of us to do. There were also lots of traditions, since we were anything but sedentary. Our day would begin with an early morning devotional and family prayer, and with a spirit of unity that lasts to this day. We owned a cabin near Park City, in Midway, and often went there on weekends. Our favorite activities were snowmobiling and sledding in the winter, and motorcycle riding, fishing, playing tennis and golf in the summer. At night, we played cards and watched videos, drank hot chocolate and in general kept ourselves going for all hours into the night.

We also had family excursions in the summertime, the most memorable being water skiing trips to Lake Powell. One time, a year or so before I was shot, I became an expert diver at Lake Powell, doing front flips off cliffs that were thirty to forty feet high. In reality, I could have easily broken my neck or back at that time. I now work with young accident victims in rehabilitation, and I am amazed that I survived those dives.

Holidays were especially exciting times for our family. Christmas and Thanksgiving topped the list. We lived for these celebrations and we were always creating new "traditions." It's ironic that I was given a shotgun for Christmas at age twelve. My siblings and I were also given a Ping-Pong table and we played a lot of table tennis. Then, after the accident, I became even more serious about it. Although I've never played table tennis in competition, I have gotten pretty good at it, even from my wheelchair.

One of the greatest legacies my parents gave me as a boy was a sheer love for being in the mountains. When people ask me what I would do for one day, if given legs to walk on, my answer is always the same, I tell them that I would spend the time running and hiking and camping in the mountains. Of course my wife would have other plans, but that's what I'd like to do! I gain almost a mystical strength whenever I spend time in the mountains, especially in the fall and in the spring. Each range is God's handiwork and being away from the pressures of life while enjoying their majesty and beauty is one of my greatest pleasures.

Chapter 5

Halloween Night, 1983 —
My Treat and Her Trick

It was a Halloween night full of promise and prospects six years after I was shot. Just before dark my friend Doug Jensen and I set out to trick or treat at the girls' dorms at Brigham Young University. We were both going to school, and having the time of our lives dating and socializing. On this particular night, as we were going from dorm to dorm, we knocked on one door that would quite literally become my door of destiny.

When the door opened, there stood one of the most beautiful persons I had ever seen. We introduced ourselves and this blonde girl named Sue invited us in. The boy she was dating had been unable to see her that evening, so she was home with her roommates, answering the door for guys like us who knew where the action was.

When we entered Sue's dorm, she thought I was all decked out in my wheelchair as part of my Halloween costume. I guess I really faked her out and when I wheeled into the living room, I immediately lifted myself out of my wheelchair and plunked myself down on the sofa. I had done this hundreds of times before, so it was no big deal. But I think it was then that she realized I really was wheelchair bound, although she didn't say anything about it.

Before long, Sue and her roommates were feeding us Captain Crunch cereal and a handful of grapes and we were laughing and having a great time. Although I was twenty-one years old, having just completed a full-time mission for my church, I was just a freshman on campus. When I met Sue, she seemed quite a bit older. But we hung out there in the dorm and although I didn't know it at the time, Sue's roommates were surprised that she was spending time with me, especially since she had a serious boyfriend. That didn't seem to bother her, though, as we hit it off pretty well.

After a while, Doug and I decided it was time to leave, so we resumed our trick or treating. The following morning, although I was unaware of it, Sue was having a conversation with about fifteen other girls in the dorm and they were all talking about "The guy in the wheelchair." We had visited them all, and evidently made a pretty good impression.

I purposely played "hard to get" for the next two weeks, but after determining to give Sue a call, I accidentally bumped into her as she was coming out of the university library. Well, I didn't literally bump into her, but I did see her and visited briefly with her at that time. I also got up the nerve to ask for her phone number and although my memory may be playing tricks on me, I recall that she actually gave it to me! She said something like, "Why don't you wheel on over?" To be truthful, she didn't say that; but she did give me her number, so I called and asked her out.

Our first date was to a pre-season BYU basketball exhibition game, in nearby Heber City. This was about twenty-five miles up the canyon from Provo and since I was the team manager, I knew it would be a good way to impress her. I was driving a 1980 two-door Pontiac J-2000 at the time, and after climbing into the driver's seat, I'd collapse my wheelchair and throw it into the seat behind me. I felt pretty heroic doing this and Sue was impressed, at least she appeared to be.

We had a good time, and visited nonstop all the way up the canyon. Because I drove my car with hand controls, I wasn't able to hold her hand. Most girls probably wish all vehicles had hand controls and I suspect she felt the same way. She was safe, her hand was safe and I just hoped she wouldn't lock her heart to having a second date.

The Big Day in American Fork, Utah.
September 2, 2000
Tami looks great and always has a place to sit.

A few years before my accident. My great grandpa, older brother Scott and younger bother Todd.

Looking to pass (or shoot) as a member of the Utah Wheelin' Jazz.

Fishing at Strawberry Reservoir with Joseph, Matthew and Kaden.

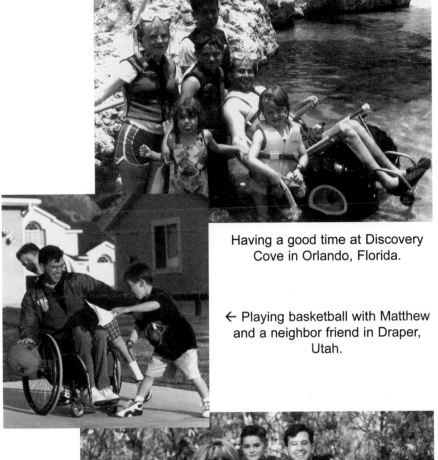

Having a good time at Discovery Cove in Orlando, Florida.

← Playing basketball with Matthew and a neighbor friend in Draper, Utah.

Tami, myself, and five unique kids.

Up to my neck in troubles in San Diego, California.

Just hanging around on a zip line in → northern Arizona.

Having fun at Cocoa Beach, Florida.

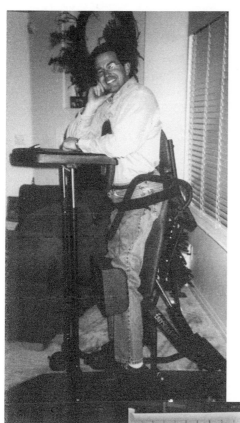

← Sometimes we have to take a stand for something.

Using my leg to push the gas on the riding lawn mower. This is proof that I do yard work.

Winning the bronze in Sydney, Australia in the 2000 Paralympics.

Our first game in the 2000 Sydney Paralympics against South Africa.

Celebrating with Mel Juette, Chuck Gill and Trooper Johnson in Sydney, Australia, 2000.

Hanging out with Dave Kiley, Chuck Gill and a crazy fan in Sydney, Australia.

Enjoying my bronze medal → and a bouquet of flowers in Sydney, Australia.

A stop at the White House to say hello to President Clinton on our way to Atlanta in 1996.

Taking a stroll with Tami.

That was about it though, since by the time the game started, I became so nauseous I could hardly hold my head up. But Sue didn't seem to mind, and somehow I made it back to Provo and dropped her off. To be truthful, I don't know if I was more relieved the date was over, or if she was. I couldn't imagine that she was impressed, especially since she thought I was sick because I was in a wheelchair. But that had nothing to do with it. I was just plain sick to my stomach.

Still, something good must have happened on our first date since not long afterward we attended a play on campus titled, "Singing Sergeants." My family met us there, so I was able to introduce them to Sue at that time. My sister-in-law, Becky, told me later that all she could think of was, "Oh, no ... another ditzy blonde!" I must have dated several of these girls, although none of them were ditzy in my mind. I dated plenty of beautiful brunettes, to be sure, but in my heart-of-hearts, I considered myself a true gentleman who preferred blondes!

Things progressed for us, and by Christmas time the fires of love were really burning. Sue returned home to her parents for the holidays and they weren't overly impressed that she was getting involved with a "boy in a wheelchair." I even sent a beautiful Bible home with her, to give them as a Christmas present. They thought it was nice, but seemed to downplay our relationship.

When the school break came to a close, I met Sue at the airport in Salt Lake City. I was wearing a tuxedo — decked out to the hilt — and we went out to a romantic candlelight dinner. It was great and the sparks were flying in both directions!

We dated steadily through the winter semester, and had the time of our lives. She was not only physically beautiful, but she had a little girl giggle and personality that was contagious. She also had the spiritual qualities I valued and that was the clincher. In short, I was smitten from head to toe and from all appearances, so was she.

I had read a saying I liked that described my determination to make Sue the object of my long term affections: "Many things in life will catch your eye, but only a few will catch your heart. Pursue those!"

And pursue I did!

During the week of final exams, Sue began to consider where she would be living in the fall. She knew she had to put down a security deposit to hold a room, and she talked with me about it. This not-so-subtle maneuver caught my attention, believe me! I suggested that she consider some other place like Wymount Terrace, a married student housing complex near campus. This was quite a romantic way to drop a hint, but she got the message, and soon we were planning how she could introduce me to her increasingly skeptical family. We decided I should fly to her home to get acquainted, and get the mystery of the wheelchair boy out in the open. So she called her mother and told her how serious we were and that she was bringing me home to "meet the family."

Sue didn't tell me this at the time, but I later learned that after getting the news that I was coming to meet the family, her mother cried for three days straight. She just couldn't accept the fact that her daughter was marrying a paraplegic. She was understandably afraid of the unknown, afraid for what her daughter might be getting into, afraid that she would have to do everything, yet never be able to bear children. I couldn't blame her, either. Even so, I really didn't see myself being different than anyone else, just doing things differently, that's all. I also had every confidence that I would one day become a father. I didn't know when, or how, but inwardly I sensed that the children we needed would be sent to us.

But things in Cleveland, Ohio, were not easy. Once out of my comfort zone, I had a difficult time doing things. While staying in her mother's home, I had to crawl upstairs, drag myself into bathrooms, and so forth. One time, in fact, Sue came to the rescue. Inviting me to wrap my arms around her neck, she hoisted me on her back and carried me up the stairs. I was worried about her hurting herself, but I was also enjoying the ride. Being that close to her was not a chore, and although her mother lifted her eyebrows when we did it, I was in seventh heaven.

Understandably, Sue's mother and father found our relationship hard to cope with. I didn't worry about it, though, because when Sunday afternoon rolled around, I did too, directly into the living room of Sue's mother's home. It was there that I proposed to her. I wanted to do wheelies when she accepted, but I contained myself, and almost before we knew it, we were engaged! It was totally awesome, and I had every confidence that her parents would come around the more they got to know me.

We've often laughed that we met on Halloween, became engaged on Easter, and got married on our anniversary. But then again, everyone gets married on their anniversary. We were falling swiftly in love, and although I was having a difficult time convincing my future in-laws that I could adequately care for their daughter, it was a time of great fun for both of us. Being with Sue was more and more intoxicating, and there was nothing I wouldn't have done for her. She made me feel like a million bucks!

Finally, on August 25, 1984, we were married in the Provo LDS temple. Sue's family traveled all the way from Ohio to be with us and it was especially fun hosting her two younger brothers, Dave and Pat. That evening we held a reception in the Provo Excelsior Hotel and more than 1,000 guests attended. It was an exhausting four-hour celebration, especially for our parents, but they went with the flow and before we knew it, we were on our honeymoon in San Diego.

And, I'll have to say, there never was a happier honeymooning couple in California! We went to the San Diego Zoo and Disneyland, enjoying the balmy tropical climate and beauty of southern California. Mostly, though, as with all honeymooners, we took time for us, exploring emotions and perspectives, and growing even deeper in love. It was a time we will always cherish, and as for me, I could hardly believe my good fortune. I had captured the woman of my dreams, the most beautiful lady in the world. What's more, I knew she loved me unconditionally and we were beginning a lifetime of laughing and loving. It was awesome!

Reflecting on how my relationship with Sue's parents and brothers had grown, I felt close to them all and appreciated how they'd grown to accept me. Even more, they respected and loved me, and this acceptance meant the world to me. As they knew, there was nothing I wouldn't do for any of them, as well as for their daughter. Next to my relationship with God, marrying Sue was truly the greatest blessing of my life and our children are a monument to our love. I appreciated more than ever Lydia Sigourney's statement that "The soul of a woman lives in love."

Looking back on our courtship and marriage, I really have to give Sue credit. Without knowing all of the issues of living with a physically disabled person, she accepted our love with a blind faith and never once looked back. I marveled at her response to our love. Two people coming together have enough issues and scripts to deal with without fashioning a marriage around a wheelchair. Add this lifelong physical limitation to the mix, and a person really has to stop and look at things from all angles. But Sue accepted me lock, stock and wheelchair. She knew she had what it took to make our marriage work and so did I. In fact, I had no doubt but that we would build a family and home life that would fulfill our every need.

Sue confirmed her commitment when she said: "Marrying anyone is taking a giant risk because we don't really know someone well enough to make such a commitment. Marrying someone who is permanently disabled involves taking a risk that is filled with uncertainty. And this is how it was with us. I wanted children more than anything in the world and I wanted a husband who could direct the course of our family with consistent, gentle leadership. Although I thought this was what I had in Mike, I didn't really know the extent of his greatness. Nor did I understand the power of faith and reliance upon the Lord in fashioning a 'forever' family."

One of the issues we had to deal with was the expression of intimacy in our marriage. While this part of our relationship was sacred and personal, we wanted to express where we're coming from. We found, like others before us, that true intimacy was emotional, and of course spiritual in nature. The physical expression, by itself, was but a vehicle, a facilitatory, that helped us become "as one." As a couple, we were fortunate in learning to be intimate in each of these ways, and our scripts and expectations were sculpted by our love and mutual admiration.

How blessed I was to have such a giving companion, and to be encircled with her love. I just hoped I would always give to her and meet her needs, as she did mine. After all, from our perspective this was what marriage was all about.

Creating a Family Script

As we married, we learned to rely upon spiritual guidance, too … especially in our desires to procreate, then to rear a family. We learned to define our relationship in a way that was fulfilling and rewarding to us both and with the help of medical science, we were blessed in bearing and rearing three beautiful children. These include Matthew, Megan and McKenzie. We loved them fiercely. What's more, we even thought they loved us. There is no greater joy than giving birth to children, then directing them along life's highways and byways. We were having the time of our lives, and we couldn't imagine a life without these beautiful kids.

I remember the night Sue told me she was expecting our first baby. She was excited to share the news with me, and all I could say was, "Wow! That's scary!" I was totally blown away with the thoughts of becoming a father, just as Sue was in anticipating her role as a mother. Matthew was finally born, and while we felt over-whelmed with the unknown challenges ahead, we couldn't have been more thrilled.

Even though I gradually matured into the role of being a dad, life was not without its difficult "fathering" moments. Still, our kids never thought of me as a "disabled dad." Of course there came an age when they realized that most dads were not in a wheelchair, but that hasn't fazed them. I do all the things fathers and their kids do together, including fishing and playing basketball, as well as playing family games such as Monopoly, Yahtzee and Clue, and although sometimes I have to do some things differently, they haven't seemed to mind.

Having two daughters was rewarding, as Megan and McKenzie both sat on my lap and combed my hair, among other father/daughter activities, and this gave me the greatest joy a father could desire. When Megan was six years old, I began having the impression that our family wasn't complete; that we were supposed to have another baby. These feelings persisted until finally I shared them with Sue. She was as surprised by them as I was. Subsequently, we returned to the doctor and announced our decision to try for one more child. We needed this fertility specialist's help and we only had the funds for a few procedures in which to have Sue become pregnant. It had taken many more times than that for our first two children to come along, but we had faith to match our limited funds, so we pressed forward.

Two weeks passed, and sure enough, we found out that Sue was, indeed, expecting our third child. We were ecstatic! Nine months later, when McKenzie was born, we knew she was a gift from heaven. She was our third miracle baby, and like the others, I could not seem to have her near me enough. Speaking of my role as a father, as I continued to deal with my physical condition, Sue observed: "One of Mike's greatest gifts is his ability to pick up on the pain of our children. It's almost like he has an antenna and can detect when one of them is experiencing negative emotions. As I've analyzed this, I think this ability has something to do with how Mike feels, himself. He is in constant pain, and so is able to empathize at a higher level than most. The kids love him for it, because he is always able to help them deal with the hurt when they have an illness or injury."

While our children have been basically healthy, they have had tubes in their ears and common problems like that. In addition, Megan had to be admitted to the Primary Children's Hospital for ten days with a sinus infection. Other than these normal occurrences, we were a healthy, action-packed family. Our biggest problem was my speaking schedule and my having to be gone so often. This gave Sue the feeling of being a "single mom," but she didn't complain. She was my biggest fan, just as I was hers, and the way we supported each other really worked.

In speaking of our children, I often told Sue that each of them has qualities I liked. I'm not just saying this, but I am continually surprised with the miniature adult that surfaces in each of them. We swam together, went snowmobiling, camping and fishing, took rides, and did about everything a family could. We loved establishing family traditions, and one of these was our annual Christmas Eve excursion to see the lights. We voted on the homes best decorated and came up with a winner every time.

But, I have to say that one of the most enjoyable things I did with the kids was to wrestle with them. They liked it, too, since they could gang up on me and pin me quite easily. They were pretty good sports about it, though, and soon got off my legs so we could have ice cream, or whatever. We were not a perfect family by any means, we had our weaknesses and our moments of frustration. Even so, were able to work through them and somehow grow even closer in the process.

Chapter 6

Striking Gold —
An Impossible Dream

Reaching for the Stars

Arriving at the ripe old age of twenty-five, I found myself loving to play basketball every bit as much as I did as a young boy. What's more, I had become pretty good at it. I loved to dribble, pass and shoot. I continued to sharpen my skills until I could dribble behind my wheelchair. and shoot three pointers.

I've heard it said that you will miss one hundred percent of the shots you don't take, and I believe it. So I became a "shooting point guard," relying on my upper-body strength to get the ball through the hoop. I knew the game was identical to the college and pro game, ten-feet high baskets, a three-point line, fouling, and so forth. The only difference I could see was that we used rubber tires instead of gym shoes. While not wanting to appear boastful, the intensity and skills required of players is also the same.

So it was with this background that I began to inquire about "trying out" for the U.S. Paralympic basketball team. The Paralympics are the second largest sporting event in the world, a sister organization to the Olympics consisting of athletes with physical disabilities. The Paralympics are held in conjunction with the Olympics, only one week later, and always in the same city. I was pursuing my Masters of Business Administration at Arizona State at this time, and the tryouts were being held in nearby Tucson.

The top sixty wheelchair basketball players in the United States were invited to try out.

I gave it my best shot (pardon the pun), and although I didn't really appreciate the odds against me at the time, I was good enough to make the team. I was the youngest player to be selected, and I was ecstatic in being able to compete in the Seoul, South Korea Paralympics.

As an interesting sidelight, when I went to try out for the Paralympic team, I found that not just paraplegic athletes competed. Some were amputees, while others had spina bifida and other physical limitations. Many of these great athletes don't live in a wheelchair, but use one only to compete. This was something I had to think about and I will bring it up later.

Arriving in Seoul

When we arrived in Korea, a bus was at the airport to escort us to the Olympic Village, and we were accompanied by armed guards. I had quite a lump in my throat, and I could hardly wait for our team to begin its first practice. The games finally began, and before I knew it we were in the gold medal game, playing against the highly touted Netherlands. Although I was the only rookie on the team, I was the starting point guard and averaged about ten points a game.

During the half-time chalk talk, it really hit home to me the a quality of the event I was participating in. This wasn't a second rate display of talent, but a game involving the finest athletes in the world. What's more, they were athletes who, in every case, had overcome tremendous personal difficulties before joining the team. I knew at that moment that I had finally realized my dream. I was playing for the greatest trophy offered, and what's more, I was confident we could win.

And win we did, with a final score of 55–43. I was happy to have scored eight points, but I was even more pleased with how well our team had performed together. Just as in life, with a corporation, or even a family, we had mastered the "team" concept. Selfishness and grandstanding had been eliminated, we had each played our role and our team had achieved the highest level of success.

Twenty minutes after winning the gold, we rolled out to listen to the national anthem while we were each presented our medal. At that moment, I experienced emotions that are impossible to put into words. Only Olympic and Paralympic athletes receiving the gold medal can possibly comprehend it. The best way I can put it is to say winning is overcoming that person inside of us who wants to quit.

Reflecting on this singular experience of my first Paralympic competition, one of the most meaningful insights I gained was in watching other disabled athletes perform on this level. My sensitivity to them, as a whole, actually began in San Francisco, when the United States team was boarding the plane for Korea. Here I was, surrounded with 600 disabled individuals who had trained themselves to become the best.

It took four hours to load the athletes and their equipment on the two airplanes. The flight attendants were patient and reminded us to stay seated, as if most of us had a choice.

Speaking of travel in general, I always try to show up late for boarding so the flight attendant, in an effort to avoid delays, will just have me sit in an empty "first class" seat. When this happens, I have a great flight, enjoying the bennies to my heart's content.

Then there is the point of arrival. When the plane pulls into its assigned gate, the flight attendant will welcome everyone to the city, then remind those who need "special assistance" to remain seated until everyone else has exited the plane. I always chuckle when this request is made of someone who spends his entire life "remaining seated!"

The next fourteen hours with my exceptional peers was an eye-opener I'll never forget. They were athletes with every disability imaginable. These included dwarfs, blind athletes, amputees, and persons who in one way or another had overcome a severe disability. This experience expanded my perspective and filled me with deep emotions. I came away from the games with an eternally altered mind-set of my own condition. I was blessed beyond measure.

One of the first friends I made after arriving at the Olympic Village was a dwarf fellow from France. He had a great sense of humor, and because I felt taller than he, we hung out a lot together. He was an eighty-pound weightlifter who bench-pressed three hundred pounds. Another of my friends — who is also a dwarf — once told me that he originally had aspirations of becoming a professional football player. Then, realizing his size limitations, he adjusted his goals to simply becoming an NFL official-size football. He was great and loved to have fun.

One day my Paralympic teammates and I decided to have a good laugh. So we encouraged our small French dwarf friend to climb inside a pillowcase in our dorm. We then hid behind the corner while the maid came to clean the room. When she got to the pillows, she "shook him out," and was she ever surprised to see him! She didn't speak English, but did she ever express herself!

We all laughed, our dwarf friend jumped down off the bed to join us and we were off to have a great day. Those moments will last forever in my mind, and were as much a part of the Paralympics as was the competition.

But speaking of the athletes' various disabilities, I should make it clear that we were not participating in the Special Olympics, the games held for the mentally disabled. Their games are held separate and apart from ours and I enjoy watching them compete.

Let me briefly share two of the most poignant moments in the 1988 Seoul Paralympics. If you can believe it, I watched a man with one leg high jump seven feet. If that wasn't spectacular enough, I saw a team of blind athletes play a game called goal ball. Similar to soccer, the ball was electronically programmed to regularly "beep" so that the team members could locate the ball and kick it. This experience was absolutely incredible and I thought I was athletic!

But I also came home with the strong conviction that Olympic success is always preceded by Olympic motivation. This was demonstrated by dozens of players I got to know.

Sharing with Others

After I returned home, my mom was so proud of my gold medal that she wanted to have it bronzed! Bronzed? I could hardly believe it, but I talked her out of this nonsense and she later had it encased in a gold display frame. I didn't really care for this, though, so I took it out and carried it around with me. I didn't do it to show off, but simply to let young kids touch it, to inspire them with the goals they could reach if they worked long and hard enough. I simply wanted to share this unusual moment in history when I played with the best wheelchair athletes in the world and this was my way of doing it.

Still, in spite of winning the medal, my greatest memories were of the journey to the Paralympics, rather than of taking the gold. It was one of the most intense and action-packed journeys imaginable, one that I'll never forget.

My Second Paralympics — With a Twist of Fate

Four years after competing in Seoul, I found myself again on an airplane. Only this time I was traveling with my teammates to Barcelona, Spain. It was to be a competition of destiny, only it wasn't the kind of destiny I had hoped for. The games in Barcelona had been heralded by the media as the best Olympics and Paralympics in Olympic history.

Things went our way once again, and finally we found ourselves accepting gold medals while the national anthem was playing and the flag was raised. We had once more gone all the way, again beating the Netherlands by three points. Little did any of us expect that not long after we returned to our homes, we would receive a letter in the mail stating that we had to give our medals back, or we would be barred from competition for life.

The Paralympic officials had randomly selected one of our star players for a drug test, and he had tested positive. He had taken a painkilling drug that, while illegal to use at the time, is now legal for certain athletes to use in Paralympic competition. None of us suspected a violation at the time, so sending our medals back, after having worked our hearts out to receive them, was one of the most difficult things I have ever done.

Perhaps I should add that as a team we petitioned the committee, then went through the courts, in vain, all in an effort to force the committee to be reasonable. Even so, the law was the law, and even though this player hadn't taken illegal drugs we still had our medals stripped from us.

While I don't harbor negative feelings about this friend and teammate whose actions inadvertently caused us to lose our gold medals, still I feel badly that one man's actions in two minutes overruled several thousand hours of work and sacrifice to achieve a goal, and that hurt. So, while this initially was a negative thing in my life, I have since used it as a tool to learn from, to dig even deeper in resolve so that I could again capture the dream I originally had. I've also come to appreciate that if life is always "rosy," and if we never lose anything, we will likewise never appreciate the good things that happen.

I have purposely told this story without using this friend's name. I didn't want his reputation tarnished in any way. But now I would like to tell you who he is. His name is Dave Kiley, and he is considered by all to be one of the greatest wheelchair basketball players ever. Nor does the story end there. After the United States team was stripped of the gold medals, Dave spent hundreds of hours trying to have the committee's decision reversed. He was devastated when this didn't happen, as were we, and he demonstrated his sterling qualities by becoming Commissioner of the National Wheelchair Basketball Association (NWBA). He is a great example of using positive energy, rather than negative, when something unexpected and undesirable takes place.

As an indicator of how Dave has helped our sport to grow, in February of 1998, he lobbied the National Basketball Association and for the first time ever we were invited to compete as part of the NBA All-Star weekend. Our game was held on Thursday evening and as a team we had the time of our lives. There were several thousand spectators and the West (our team) beat the East team by a score of 78-73.

There is a certain irony, I believe, in Dave's story that was expressed by W. H. Beecher when he wrote "Not what men do worthily, but what they do successfully, is what history makes haste to record." Dave was both worthy and successful.

My Third Paralympics

Reflecting on my seemingly never-ending basketball saga, I made the Paralympic wheelchair basketball team again in 1996. This time the games were to be held in Atlanta, Georgia. Because of my previous two competitions, I was going as a veteran and I was going to have fun! While obtaining a gold medal was my personal goal, the Paralympic experience had grown deeply valuable to me. From experience, I knew that rubbing shoulders with, and learning from, the great athletes of the world, would give me perspective and a further insight. What's more, although my wife Sue had gone to the first two Paralympics with me, this time we would be taking Matthew, and that was something special. He wouldn't remain for the entire games, of course, but it was an experience we would remember as a family and this gave an entirely new meaning to it.

What I didn't know until competition time was that I was about to learn a lesson of an entirely different color. We progressed undefeated, pretty much as we had expected to. Then, in the semi-finals, we played Australia. We knew that if we beat them, we would play Great Britain for the gold the following evening. While we led through much of the game, one of Australia's players, Troy Sachs, had the game of his career scoring forty-two points, and we ended up losing by a single point. It was nothing less than horrible for us and most of the 10,000 spectators, especially since we knew we should have beaten them!

Following the game, the locker room was pandemonium! Wheelchairs, both empty and with others sitting in them, were flying everywhere, along with cursing and yelling and unbridled anger! It was a scene I'll never forget! We just didn't know how to lose; but because I was the only player on the team who had competed and won medals in the previous two Paralympics, it was easier for me to take our loss in stride. Our coach, Brad Hedrick, finally gave a very emotional speech and that seemed to settle our emotions and prepare us for our final game.

This meant that we would play Spain for the bronze medal and we won this game quite handily. It was different taking third, but it was also very gratifying. The one consolation in winning a bronze medal instead of a silver medal is that at least the players return home having won the final game.

Since receiving this medal, I've had fun showing it to people, especially the braille inscription on the back for the blind athletes. While rubbing this inscription, I tell people that it says something like "Australia kicked your butt. Better luck next time!" The moral of this story is be a winner, not a whiner!

During the medal ceremony, I honestly didn't have animosity toward the team that had beaten us the day before and was now accepting the gold. They deserved to win and had done it fair and square. In a way, I was happy for them because I had sat in their chairs twice before, and I knew what they were experiencing. I also knew we were winners, even with a bronze medal. Winning any Olympic or Paralympic medal was the dream of a lifetime, so knowing my family was there to celebrate this moment with me made it all worthwhile. Although the bronze is certainly nothing to be ashamed of, I will always believe that if we had paid just a bit more attention to detail, we would have and should have won the gold. I guess one never knows, and that's why the game is played. Even so, deep inside I knew I'd be on hand for one more try at Olympic gold four years later!

An Unprecedented Fourth Paralympics

Because the Aussies had beaten us in Atlanta, I had an even greater motivation to make the team and beat them on their home court. Fortunately, I was selected to represent the U.S.A. in Sidney for the 2000 Paralympics. I would be one of only two or three wheelchair basketball players to have competed in four Paralympics. This is not to assert that I was trying to be better than others. That couldn't be further from the truth. But I have had the inner goal of participating in four Paralympics for as long as I could remember. I simply wanted to achieve my greatest potential as an athlete, just as I've determined to do so in life — both as a professional and as the head of a happy, successful family.

What I had no way of knowing was that within weeks my entire life would turn upside-down. This would happen unexpectedly and shake me to the very core.

Chapter 7

Agency and Compensation, Two Very Pivotal Concepts

The Law of Agency

Going through a divorce was something I never once thought would happen to me and my family. But we all have our agency. Still, personal agency has its rewards and its costs, depending on the decisions we make. The bottom line is that we're held accountable.

I learned a great deal about the idea of agency four years ago when my wife informed me that she was no longer in love with me, and wanted to end our 15-year marriage. Out of respect for her, I won't share the details. I'll simply say that I was stunned, then deeply depressed. I knew that I was not blameless in the breakdown of our marriage and I had made my own mistakes, but I worked my tail off for a different conclusion than what eventually took place.

Finally, my wife's decision became permanent. After meeting with our three children, I became resigned to having a broken family. I assured our kids that both of their parents still loved them dearly and that even though we would be living in two different households, we would continue to have the same "mom and dad relationship" with them.

There is no need to pretend that the divorce has not taken its toll on our children, for it has. Still, they respect their mother and her change of feelings and that is as it should be. I made a commitment to them to never speak ill, or judgmentally, of their mother and I will honor that promise for as long as I live.

So I moved out, then began to be a "father" from a distance. Sue soon remarried and our children were immediately thrust into a blended family. Her new husband had been our neighbor and one of my best friends. He was a good man and I deeply prayed that his influence on our children would be positive.

Learning the Principle of Compensation

One of my religious leaders taught me something I firmly believe. It is that, when something unpleasant or unearned happens to a person, the Lord in His tender mercy brings a compensating blessing. In my case, this blessing came in a package of "three" and arrived when I was experiencing my darkest hour.

One day, as the ripples of divorce gradually subsided, my sister Collette spoke to me about one of her closest friends — a new widow and mother of two. Her name was Tami Gibbons and she was Collette's neighbor. At the time, I felt badly for the trials Collette's friend had been through and I hoped the best for her.

Tami had been happily married to her husband, Rich, and together they had brought Joseph, Robbie, and Anna into their home. Robbie, however, had been born with a congenital heart defect. After open-heart surgeries and many traumatic days dealing with his pain, he passed away in 1996. He had just celebrated his second birthday and his death had been a blow to Tami's family.

As if this weren't enough, just before Robbie passed away, Tami's husband, Rich, discovered that he had a brain tumor. Although the tumor was inoperable, Rich and Tami tried every form of alternative medicine to arrest the tumor and prolong his life.

Their efforts were futile, however, and after a continuous degeneration, Rich passed away in 1998. Adding to Tami's difficulties, she was nine months pregnant with their baby at the time of her husband's funeral. The day after he was buried, Tami went into labor and gave birth to their third child, a beautiful girl she named Anna Richey.

I certainly could sympathize with her and knew, as in my own case, that the old saying, "Things turn out best for those who make the best of the way things turn out," was often hard to swallow.

For Tami and her two living children the next year was extremely lonely and difficult. Her family gave their total support, but still it was hard for her.

By this time I had moved to Orem, and was living with my parents. Tami was living four houses away from my sister, in nearby Pleasant Grove and after visiting my sister and seeing Tami's family Christmas picture on the refrigerator, I knew I wanted to meet that woman. Our meeting did not take place for several more months.

At last we did on March 28, 1999. That evening I anxiously attended a church choir concert. Tami, with her musical talents, was the director.

Afterward, Tami walked into the foyer. I was there with my three children and my parents. Soon everyone "conveniently" left the building, so it became the perfect time to become acquainted with the lady I was dying to meet.

Moments before, my son, Matt, had gone home with my folks, taking the key to my van with him. This left me stranded. Seeing that I had no transportation home, Tami offered to take me home. She had to put my wheelchair in her van and I felt more helpless than ever. But she was very capable, a care giver of the first order and I watched how effortlessly she helped me out.

I couldn't have been more impressed with Tami. She was stunningly beautiful, her mind was deep and engaging, and she laughed and joked like we'd known each other for a lifetime. Our personalities meshed and within two months we were engaged. We were both prayerful — and careful — about this decision and we felt sure of ourselves.

What we couldn't have anticipated, of course, was the roller coaster ride our relationship would experience over the next 18 months. I wasn't ready to get married again. The pain of divorce was so deep that I needed time. Tami understood, and although we were "on and off again," we always came back to each other. I needed to date other women, which I did, and every time Tami came out the winner. Maybe I should say that I came out the winner because of the strength of my feelings for her. I never questioned her love for me, or her loyalty.

"The final straw," Tami remembers, "was the annual July 4th Stadium of Fire celebration at Brigham Young University. I went with a date and we took my son Joseph and two of his cousins.

"As we were walking around the stadium, looking for something to eat, we saw Mike. It had been six weeks since he and I had broken up and I was not prepared for what happened next. I saw Mike from a distance and suddenly I had a hard time breathing. Joseph saw him in the same instant, and ran up to him to give him a big hug. Mike was buying pizza for himself and was all smiles.

"It was very awkward for my date who was ordering pizza, but I had to give Mike a quick hug, too. We chatted for a minute, at which time my date walked over to ask me if two pieces of pizza would be enough.

"Mike was as surprised as I was. After all, he thought that *he* was the only one who could date others. So, we said goodbye and went back into the stadium to watch the show. However, I don't think either Mike or I enjoyed the fireworks. I had chills and couldn't stop shaking for what seemed like forever."

I was surprised to see Tami and her kids. She was more beautiful than ever and I realized how much I missed her. I didn't know how serious she was about the guy she was with, so I thought I'd waste no time in finding out.

I had recently purchased a home in Draper, near my children. My friend, Nick Hess, was living with me in my basement apartment, so later that night I drove all the way back home to drop him off. Then, with Tami on my radar, I turned around and drove all the way back to Pleasant Grove.

When I pulled up to the curb in front of Tami's home, I called her on my cell phone. It was 1:00 A.M., but I didn't care. I needed to talk to her and see where she and I stood.

Tami answered the phone. When I told her I was parked outside her home, she invited me inside. We talked, and I told her how long the past six weeks had been for me. She had experienced the same feelings. Before long, we were in each other's arms kissing. Our emotions were pretty intense and the weeks being apart melted in minutes.

After a long talk — and several more kisses — I finally went home. I was re-committed to our relationship. She was as well. Having both been married before we were willing to speak with a counselor about how we could deepen our relationship.

Reflecting on this time, Tami says, "Some of my family and friends were apprehensive that I was marrying a man with a disability. But I wasn't concerned. After meeting Mike, from day one his chair was never an issue. I loved Mike for the incredible man he was, day in and day out a model of perseverance, determination and a positive attitude. Most important, I was *in love* with him. I was attracted to him, and I loved his smile!"

During this period of new commitment, I invited Tami and her kids to come with my family to the Schlappi Family Reunion. It was being held at Camelot Campgrounds near Strawberry Reservoir. The Uintah mountains in northern Utah were beautiful.

Tami's verdict after meeting my family is best told in her own words: "I loved Mike's entire family and had known them for over a year. So it was great feeling as if I was part of them. I wanted to be a member of that family for so long!"

The day of the reunion finally arrived — July 28, 2000. Everyone gathered at the fishing pond that Collette had arranged for the kids. It was the kind of pond where a child throws a line over a sheet, then waits. When there is a tug on the line, the child pulls it back and finds a prize at the end of the line.

Remembering that fateful fishing hole, Tami adds, "I got a late start. I was still back at camp when Mike's sister-in-law, Becky, came to find me. She insisted that I hurry down to the fishing pond immediately.

"I didn't think anything of her request ... that is, not until everyone prodded *me* to fish. When I finally said I would, I noticed Collette's husband, Troy, hiding behind a tree with a camera. My heart started to pound as I considered what might be on the end of my line. Seconds passed, and sure enough — when I pulled my line over the sheet, I saw I had caught a little green box! With all eyes on me, I began to cry. My kids didn't have a clue as to what I was crying about. I opened the box and saw a ring that was so much more than I deserved, and *so* beautiful."

Tami was excited alright, but no more than I was. My heart was beating a hundred miles an hour and I soon found myself putting the ring on her finger. It seemed to fit perfectly, too, and the real celebrating then took place.

Within sixty days, Tami and I were married. We went to Lake Tahoe for our honeymoon and it couldn't have been more rewarding for both of us. We were truly in love. I was more than compensated for the loss of my first marriage and she was for the loss of her husband. The Lord had answered my prayers and although we would go through difficult times, blending our separate family scripts, I had every confidence that we would build a solid marriage.

"I had been through a great deal," Tami said, "but I believed in prayer. Mike and his children were the answer to my prayer and all our children get along great together. After all our two families had been through, our lives were again filled with happiness."

Personally Speaking

Perhaps the greatest secret to the vitality of our marriage has been our ability to share feelings. Not simply to express thoughts, as most couples do, but to get down to the nitty-gritty and express how we feel about something. I'm sure my disability has contributed to our need to communicate — another one of those unexpected benefits — but nonetheless, we've grown close because we talk things out, and that's made all the difference. We share, and we care. Oh, marriage hasn't been without its moments, that's for sure. In fact, for both of us it's the hardest thing we've ever tried to do. But we work as a team perhaps because we've been forced to do so. This is a nugget of gold that we've discovered, and we wouldn't trade it for anything.

We have found it intriguing, over the years, that people want to focus on the more personal part of our marriage. Whenever we meet someone, we've almost come to expect that they have two questions: First, can we have sex? And second, are our children ours? We're not defensive about these questions because we know the inquisitive nature of human beings. Sensing their thoughts, and listening at times to their queries, we politely explain that we couldn't be happier in our marriage. We then say, "Yes, they're our kids by our mutual love and affection for them."

But our success, both as contributing adults to society, as well as a husband and wife team that is doing its best to rear children with values and aspirations, is measured by the joy we experience each day we live. We're home bodies, and we love it, even though we're always on the run, looking for things to do and friends to do them with. Although my speaking engagements and sports competitions force me to travel a great deal, we've adapted to this regimen, and live for the times we're together. This, after all, is the greatest success a person can experience.

Heading for Australia

Not long after we were married my dream of participating in a fourth Paralympics became a reality. Tami and I decided to make it a second honeymoon. I left early for Sydney, Australia, and worked out with my team in order to become acclimated to the time change. Being away from Tami was difficult, but we spoke regularly on the phone and I knew she would soon be with me.

"Being away from each other was hard on me," Tami said. "I continued to be the 'mom' at home, but I had heard so much about the Olympic experience and felt badly I was not there for every minute of it.

"I didn't feel I could leave my kids for too long, so I was planning to miss the opening ceremonies and the first game. Still I was torn because I wanted to experience the *whole* thing with Mike. I had only heard about his other Paralympic games, and now it was a chance for me to experience them first-hand.

"When Mike at last called, we both decided I would fly to Australia early, and enjoy the opening festivities as well as every game on the schedule. As it turned out, arriving for the Opening Ceremonies was the best birthday present I could have asked for."

Tami, my parents, and other family members, finally arrived for the games. Having them with me meant everything. They had to stay in a little out-of-the-way motel, while I stayed in the Olympic Village with my team. It was definitely not the way I wanted our reunion to be. Of course, I will admit I sneaked Tami into Olympic Village on one or two occasions.

"When I finally arrived at the Paralympics Opening Ceremony," Tami recalled, "I was so excited I could hardly stand it. I hadn't seen Mike yet, and with more than 120,000 spectators in the stadium, I wondered if I would be able to find him so that I could get my ticket.

"The U.S.A. athletes were some of the last ones to enter the stadium. The basketball players were all lined up in their red, white and blue chairs ready to roll into the opening ceremonies.

"I was so excited when I saw Mike that I ran and jumped onto his lap, straddling his chair. I gave him the biggest hug of his life! I didn't want to let go, but after a few seconds, I heard the U.S.A. team chanting, 'Tami, Tami, Tami,...' We were kissing and hugging and I was in seventh heaven being there with Mike."

Seeing Tami was the best. We'd only been apart for ten days, but it seemed like an eternity. Having her at the games made all the difference for me, even if we couldn't stay together all of the time.

As we prepared to play our first game against the team from South Africa, I could hardly wait. Between practices I had time to consider the little bit of history I was making. I was going to be the first basketball player to participate in four consecutive Paralympics, and this gave me a lot of satisfaction. Training had been difficult, especially while I was trying to regain control of my life. But all that was behind me and I was in ecstasy.

Looking Back

Reflecting on my own experience, and how my game of basketball evolved, I actually began playing competitive sports in the community Bantam League. I played baseball, basketball, and football and loved them all. What made things even more fun, as I got into basketball, was that my dad was always my coach. He was great, too, a real people builder, and with his encouragement, I knew I could do anything! It was awesome! What's more, my mom was always at my games, cheering me on. Both parents had their own way of motivating me and I would have died trying to perform to their expectations.

I need to mention that I wasn't just a pampered kid who spent his summers attending one basketball camp after another. Instead, my dad ingrained within my mind the need to practice hard all the time so that I could get ahead of my competition. His work ethic became mine and I knew only one speed, fast forward!

I love a statement made by Edwin Markham because it reflects so truly what I believe: "That which we persist in doing becomes easier to do; not that the nature of the thing has changed, but that our ability to do it has increased."

To illustrate how intense I was about competition, I remember many times getting up in the wintertime, shoveling snow off our neighbor's driveway, then putting on my gloves and shooting baskets for an hour to an hour-and-a-half. This I did in the early morning, prior to heading off to school. I really did want to get ahead of my competition, although I like to think that I also wanted to be the best "Mike" I could possibly be.

Part of my motivation to excel came from a kid in the neighborhood by the name of Kirby Johnson. He was not a particularly gifted athlete, but he would literally practice basketball four or five hours a day. He was consumed with the desire to play in the NBA, and his work ethic showed it. The best part of this for me was the fact that I always had someone to play basketball with. Because my dad was a former high school coach, I had the basics down, so spending so many hours with Kirby turned out to be a great benefit to me.

To summarize my life's experience with competition, I believe I have unquestionably accomplished more because of it. To be even more explicit, I have always tried to compete with myself, rather than with others. Competing, in and of itself, is rather shallow ... if all a person wants to do is "beat out" the competitor. Challenging oneself, then having the dogged dedication to train at one's highest possible level is really what makes it worthwhile.

Let the Games Begin

The Paralympic Games of 2000 soon began and our team found ourselves facing a formidable team from South Africa. I was named starting guard, as I had been in former games, and I couldn't have been more psyched. I was also excited for another reason. Dave Kiley, my former teammate whose positive blood test had cost us the gold medal in Spain, was again on the team. He had paid heavy dues to redeem himself, including being banned from participating in the Atlanta Paralympics. Now, however, all that was behind him and we were having a great time together.

Our team won the first game and my stats were good. I had twelve points, seven rebounds, six assists, and three steals. Unfortunately, as the games progressed, I spent fewer and fewer minutes on the court. The younger players progressed in confidence and experience and we advanced all the way to the medal rounds. Not playing as much as I was used to was hard for me, but I decided to not let it bother me. When I wasn't playing, I would sit back and take in the experience. It couldn't have been more rewarding.

We finally got down to the semi-finals, and played Holland's team. Things didn't go our way, however, and by halftime we were down by 14 points. In the closing minutes of the second half, we pulled up to within two points. My teammate took a three-point shot at the buzzer for the win, but it wasn't meant to be. So we found ourselves once again playing for a bronze medal.

We were devastated, to say the least, just as in the previous Paralympics. The guys were crying right along with the coach. It was especially hard since we had won the World Championship two years earlier. Seeded Number One, we were the favorites going into the games.

The next day we were scheduled to play Great Britain for the bronze medal and it was an agonizing, sleepless night. We didn't know how we would get back "up" to win, but somehow we psyched each other up and mentally prepared for the game.

The medal games were noise-wracking. There were 20,000 paying fans in the stands, each of them yelling for his team. Earlier in the tournament we had beaten Great Britain in overtime, so we knew we were in for a dog fight.

The game progressed and became more intense. I already had two gold and one bronze medal and I wanted one more. After all, I had become a collector of "heavy metal." I wanted to return to my home in Utah as a four-time Paralympic medalist. It was the goal I had worked for all of my life.

With 25 seconds to go in the game the score was tied. The crowd was totally out of control and my heart was in my throat. I had only played about ten minutes of the game, but all my energy was focused on winning. Suddenly Great Britain's coach called time-out. They had the ball and we had one foul to give, so I was telling the guys to hurry and foul so we would get the ball back, but they couldn't hear.

About 17 seconds went by before one of Great Britain's players drove in for a lay-up. He missed, and we grabbed the rebound. Barreling down the court with the ball, one of our young players, Paul Schulte, let the ball fly from almost half court. He heaved the shot from 30–35 feet, which is an impossible shot for someone sitting in a wheelchair. The ball arched through the air, and "swoosh!" … nothing but the bottom of the net as the buzzer sounded!

I leaped off the bench in my wheelchair, rolled across the floor, then jumped into the pile as pandemonium erupted and I was instantly on the bottom of the pile. My knees were upside-down in the photo that appeared in the next day's paper, but I didn't care. I was there to be part of it. Tami and my family were with me, and I had never been so thrilled.

The place went nuts. I was amazed to be so happy … a very different emotion than the other time we had won bronze. This time we hadn't *lost* the gold, but had *won* the bronze. I had an entirely different mind-set.

Soon we were receiving our medals and I was silently thanking Heavenly Father for giving me such a rich experience. Four Paralympics representing the United States. How could I have been more blessed?

Afterward, when we were flying home I finally had a chance to sit back and analyze my life. It had taken unexpected turns, to be sure, but I had a beautiful wife and five children who called me

Dad. My faith, both in God and myself, couldn't have been stronger. Even more important, I knew that whatever happened next I was prepared to handle it.

Chapter 8

Securing Success Through Adversity
— Six Bulletproof Principles for
Personal Success

Throughout my life, and especially after my accident, I've had a penchant for not exposing my weaknesses. I'm sure being in a wheelchair has made me more sensitive to this than I may have been otherwise, but nonetheless it's true. I have a yearning that comes from deep within, and it is to succeed at the highest levels. While I am limited to what I can accomplish physically, I have never felt limited as to what I can do overall. If anything, people have called me an over achiever. I've accomplished whatever I've set out to do, and that includes serving a full-time mission for my church, graduating from college, receiving an M.B.A. at Arizona State University and being a successful inspirational speaker and businessman.

I certainly do not mean to share these accomplishments in a boastful manner, for if anything, I give credit to Tami and others, and of course, to God, for supporting me along the way. I fervently believe in the power of the mind and in living with great expectations. Also I have lived by the motto: *If we resist change, we'll fail, if we accept change, we'll survive; and if we create change, we'll succeed.* To accomplish great expectations, I have developed six bulletproof principles I would now like to share. After all, these have become my "keys to freedom," and to ensure a successful, action-packed life.

Six Bulletproof Principles for Success

Principle Number One: Live to grow and to change, rather than merely to "exist." In other words, tackle life with a passion! I first realized this need almost immediately after I had been shot. At that time, my lens was cloudy, and I had to find a suitable "mental Windex" to regain clarity of vision. This clarity literally began with my decision to get up every morning. There was no pressure to do this, so I had to dig deep down inside and create the pressure. Becoming passionate was the result. It was "mind over mattress" of the first order!

The opposite of living with passion is simply giving up, allowing someone to push our "kill" button. Many people die at age seventy-five who stopped living at age thirty. From my experience, this is a disease fostered by low self-esteem.

When I was younger and newly injured, I began competing in marathons. I loved the challenge and although I always fell behind at the beginning uphill portion of the race, I passed most of the runners on the downhill stretch. One day, while competing in the Deseret News Marathon, I realized that participating in a lengthy race like this was much like life. At the beginning, people are there to cheer us on and encourage our efforts. Likewise, thousands are there to cheer us across the finish line. The difficult part, the twenty-six miles of asphalt in between, is where the measure of a man is made. Although we always appreciate support from others, in the final sum of things, our own decisions determine our outcome.

Principle Number Two: Learn to take responsibility for our attitudes and our actions! That is, rather than project blame, or to allow the seeds of anger and discontent to enter our hearts when something goes wrong, we should be "in control" of our emotional response. The first cousin to this idea is the need we have to set goals, to create a life map. After all, corporations have mission statements, so why shouldn't individuals? The person who expects nothing from him or herself will certainly never be disappointed.

A recent example of this notion is the disabled pro golfer, Casey Martin. Because of Casey's extremely atrophied leg, a judge in Eugene, Oregon recently made it possible for him to ride a cart on the pro golf tour. As reported in our daily newspaper *The Herald,* "For Martin, the landmark ruling was not just a victory for him; it was a symbolic victory for all those with a disability who have been told they can't. 'I realized if I win, [Martin was quoted as saying] it would open the way. That's something to feel good about.'"

Not only has twenty-five-year-old Casey Martin excelled in his sport by winning a PGA tournament in Lakeland, Florida, just weeks before this court ruling, but he is living within his limitations while invoking the Americans with Disabilities Act to allow him to compete on the professional level he has worked so hard to achieve. It is a great victory for one who has taken responsibility for his own future.

Principle Number Three: Live not only to accept adversity, but to relish the acceptance of it. After all, the finest steel is made in the hottest furnaces. I call this strategy welcoming the "refiner's fire."

A year following my accident, Torrey and I were hanging out at the local mall and having a good time. Even so, I could tell that everyone who passed looked at me with a curious eye. At the time, I didn't like it and I wanted to put a sign on my chest that read: *I got shot, you geek! What's your problem?*

Although it may seem contrived, we actually had a lady come up to us and ask me why I was in a wheelchair. My response was awkward, but I simply and truthfully said, "Because my friend here shot me." He and I laughed, but that lady surely didn't.

After returning home that afternoon, I began to realize that people weren't being rude in looking at me or asking about my condition. They were simply being curious. I then realized that the way I carried myself was going to be the way they would regard me. They would either see me as a person with a personality, or as a paraplegic who was impaired. It was at this moment of discovery that I determined to not only accept my adversity, but to relish the acceptance of it!

Principle Number Four: Live with a "Service Mentality." From what I've seen, life is made up of takers and givers, those who scavenge from society, and those who contribute. While providing a living is important, what's even more essential is to serve others. Today's hedonistic society is all too selfish and that's frightening. If I can be remembered for anything, it would be that "Mike cared."

An adjunct to this idea of serving others is to do it "positively." Ken Blanchard, the popular author and training and development instructor once wrote a one-minute course in public speaking. In it, he states, "Of all the concepts I have taught over the years, the most important is about 'catching people doing things right.' There is little doubt in my mind that the key to influencing people is to catch them doing something right, then praising them for their performance."

I've heard it said that no one cares how much we know until they know how much we care. We care by lifting and genuinely praising others, rather than confronting and condemning them. This, after all, is the only way to serve!

Principle Number Five: Live for a family, rather than just "with" one. The greatest success I've had, of course, is with my family. Both Tami and I feel that the family, rather than the individual, or the village, is the basic unit of society, and that greater joy can come from this experience than from any other episode life could present.

Permit me to share a memo I recently received which reported a true story from the Vietnam war. I call it "packing parachutes."

Charles Plumb, a U.S. Naval Academy graduate, was a jet fighter pilot in this war. After seventy-five combat missions, his plane was destroyed by a surface-to-air missile. Plumb ejected and parachuted into enemy hands. He was captured and spent six years in a communist prison. But he survived, and is alive to tell about it today.

One day, when Plumb and his wife were sitting in a restaurant, a man at another table came up and said, "You're Plumb! You flew jet fighters in Viet Nam from the aircraft carrier Kitty Hawk. You were shot down!"

"How in the world did you know that?" asked Plumb

"I packed your parachute," the man replied proudly. Plumb gasped in surprise and gratitude. The man pumped his hand and said, "I guess it worked!"

Assuring him, Plumb replied, "It sure did. If your chute hadn't worked, I wouldn't be here today."

Plumb couldn't sleep that night, thinking about that man. Of that night, he observed, "I kept wondering what he might have looked like in a Navy uniform, a Dixie cup hat, a bib in the back, and bell bottom trousers. I wondered how many times I might have passed him on the Kitty Hawk. I wondered how many times I might have seen him and not even said, 'Good morning, how are you?' or anything because, you see, I was a fighter pilot and he was just a sailor."

Plumb thought of the many hours the sailor had spent on a long wooden table in the bowels of the ship, carefully weaving the shrouds and folding the silks of each chute, holding in his hands each time the fate of someone he didn't know."

When I think of Plumb, I think of how spouses and parents spend their lives packing parachutes. We spend our energies providing the means for members of the family to make it through the day. It is not only our stewardship, it is our opportunity and blessing, in fact, it is our greatest opportunity and blessing!

Principle Number Six: Learn to laugh! Life is so serious, with such great demands. We all need to lean back, stretch, and laugh!

One humorous incident took place when I was in college and before I met Tami. My friend, Doug and I wanted to spiffy up a blind double date, so I loaned him one of my wheelchairs and we both went "wheeling" up to Deseret Towers to pick up our dates. We were not only blind dates to them, but were also disabled!

The girls couldn't believe we were both disabled, but they went with us to the university bowling alley. On our way down the hill, bad luck struck! Not being practiced in the art of wheelchair riding, Doug lost control of his chair and landed directly in a window well. People came to his rescue and pulled him out, then we continued on to campus. Once there, Doug continued his charade by bowling from his chair, just as I did. This was okay until he again fell out of the chair.

Before the girls could respond and run to his rescue, he jumped to his feet, yelling, "Surprise!" They could see they'd been duped, but soon all was forgotten and we had a great time. We're not sure our two dates liked it, but we certainly did.

Another humorous situation that illustrates how one can actually have fun, even with what he has lost, is reflected in the antics of one of my Paralympic basketball teammates, Reggie Colton. He is a double amputee, and sometimes when we pre-board a plane, he'll hoist himself into one of the upper luggage bins. He is one of the strongest men I know, and just as agile. We then close the lid, only to have it opened by a startled passenger moments later. As they open the compartment, Reggie jumps out and frightens them. Maybe this is taking things a bit too far, I don't know; but I do know that in the face of personal loss a person can have a much easier time of it if he is able to laugh at himself and his situation rather than to feel sorry for himself.

Chapter 9

Thinking Differently

One of the real traps people get into is the trap of sameness. Perhaps the first thing my accident did for me was force me to think differently. I've often heard it said that we all spend our lives adjusting. In my case, I began to think that, contrary to popular belief, my wheelchair was not my identity. It was simply another tool, like my glasses and my automobile, that could help me perform at a level higher than I might otherwise have been able to do.

This "different thinking" has reached into other areas of my life, as well. Since evolving and healing from my accident, I found myself avoiding judgment of others according to outward symbols. I look inside a person's heart, as I have stated, at his or her motives, desires and attitude.

What's sad is that so many disabled people spend their lives reacting to their perception of what others think of them, rather than purposefully "doing their own thing." They won't admit to being disabled, nor will they hang around others with similar limitations. When I meet these people, I study their statements, gleaning all I can from what they have learned from their mistakes or misfortunes.

One of the special people who does his own thing is Mike Johnson. Mike is a double amputee who lost his legs and several of his fingers in a land mine explosion in the Vietnam War. He lived several miles from me and after I got used to my wheel-chair, he kept pressing me to come out of my shell and play competitive basketball. In retrospect, he was one of the most important people who helped me overcome adversity with class and with dignity.

Where from Here?

I stress the notion that individuals with disabilities should hope for the best, yet prepare for the worst. I take this motto seriously, and have great hope in my own future progress. Medical scientists are already having success in regenerating nerves and in having the spinal cord repair itself. I don't think it's far-fetched to envision a day in the not too distant future when my son and I will walk together as we tackle our favorite golf course or fishing hole, or that I can dance on my feet with my daughters at their weddings. This is my hope ... if not for me, then for others who will follow.

Life's Other Adversities

It's interesting that, when speaking to me people are often consumed with my injury, as if my disability was the only difficulty I had to contend with. These people are often surprised when I tell them that, just like themselves, I deal with all types of difficulties. Life is difficult for everyone, not just someone who lives in a wheelchair. Depression can set in when a business deal goes sour, anger and frustration can arise when others don't meet our expec-tations and so forth. I often paraphrase the bumper sticker which says: *Life's tough and then you die!*

Everyone has heartaches and disabilities, they are simply more obvious for some than others. In fact, from what I've seen, often the emotional and spiritual disabilities a person experiences far exceed any physical disability I might have. This is perhaps true because when you can't see your inner disabilities, you have little incentive to overcome them. In fact, these weaknesses often become part of the baggage retained and even "made sacred" as they are kept in a theoretical fanny pack. People take them out and display them when convenient, then quietly tuck them back out of sight as they continue their trek, all with the extra weight this excess baggage provides.

Perhaps a perfect example of this would be my friend who initially shot me. While I immediately forgave him, and meant it, to my knowledge he never forgave himself. He grew up, married, and tried to do life by his own rules. Then one day he broke the law and is now suffering greatly for his wrongs. In essence, he has at least temporarily lost all that he had worked for, including his wife and family. If he hasn't done so already, my prayer for him is that he forgive himself for the part he played in my accident. I hope that one day he'll realize how good a person he is and that he can take his place in society as a contributing, happy individual.

I firmly believe that, regardless of what people do to self-destruct, they are all looking for happiness. My nickname as a youth was "Happy Schlappi," and I wore the handle proudly. That is, until I broke up with a girlfriend. Then that particular girl would label me, "Crappy Schlappi." During those moments I was pretty down on myself. It is absolutely true that trying to find happiness from the 'outside in' is a futile task. The only true happiness comes from the 'inside out.'

I've also learned it is imperative that, along with all other habits, I internalize habits of self-progress, rather than those of self-destruction. In her *Autobiography in Five Short Chapters,* Portia Nelson provides a humorous yet insightful sequence that sums up the core challenge for attitude therapy. I share it as follows, as a setup for success, or failure, depending on our ability to proactively play life's game with the cards we are dealt:

Chapter I
I walk down the street.
There is a deep hole in the sidewalk.
I fall in
I am lost … I am helpless
It isn't my fault.
It takes me forever to find a way out.

Chapter II
I walk down the same street.
There is a deep hole in the sidewalk.
I pretend I don't see it.
I fall in again.
I can't believe I am in the same place,
It isn't my fault.
It still takes a long time to get out.

Chapter III
I walk down the same street.
There is a deep hole in the sidewalk.
I see it is there.
I still fall in … it is a habit.
My eyes are open.
I know where I am.
It is my fault.
I get out immediately.

Chapter IV
I walk down the same street.
There is a deep hole in the sidewalk.
I walk around it.

Chapter V
I walk down another street!

It is crucial that we sow seeds of constructive habits and that we internalize the personal and professional integrity to be responsible for self. We thus have the strength of conviction to turn around and change directions to avoid getting bogged down in the quicksand of self-defeating attitudes and behaviors. Personal change *is* possible and can become not only a habit, but the core of one's character. This, in the final sum of things, will allow us to reap a destiny of success, wellness, and peace. After all, it is what makes life worth living! Hopelessness and failure are the greatest disabilities and combine to introduce a plague that stretches far and wide. Hope and success, on the other hand, breed upon themselves and allow a person to enjoy a life of accomplishments, self-fulfillment, and most of all, peace.

While I have enjoyed lofty athletic ambitions and achievements, my goal at this time in my life is to take my message of Attitude Therapy and share it with the world. It is a remarkable high to be invited to speak to corporate America and to share my story. I speak with tongue-in-cheek when I say how great it is to receive a standing ovation. After all, I can't stand and join in! Seriously, in my mind I not only stand, but I race forward with an enthusiasm and energy that could not be greater! After all else, what could be more meaningful and empowering? Life has taught me: *If you can't stand up stand out!* Enough said.

For Further Information
or
To Order Additional Books:

As an inspirational speaker, Mike is motivating, uplifting and entertaining. If you would like to have him speak to your organization — contact his web site:

www.mikeschlappi.com

His business address is:

Mike Schlappi Communications
641 East Pheasant Haven
Draper, Utah 84020
Phone: 801-553-MIKE (6453)
E-mail: mike@mikeschlappi.com